Development Of A Country Is A Collective Effort:

The Case Of Ghana

Gabriel Awuah

ISBN: 978-1-4092-0192-2

To

Hannah

And

Gabriela

Preface

As far back as the 1980s, and even earlier, many people have been trying to explain why Africa has not been able to contribute significantly to the trade among the nations of the world or to improve the living standards of the majority of people in Africa. Some popular explanations for the poor performance of Africans have been: small internal markets, many countries with few natural resources, a relatively underdeveloped general infrastructure (e.g. power supplies, transportation, financial institutions, market organizations, and other environmental institutions), high foreign debts, limited possibilities for manufactured exports, over reliance on primary products, and governmental restrictions. It was no wonder then that in the 1980s the world bodies started seriously to realize that most of the loans and the development help given to many African countries had not been bearing fruits as had been expected. For example, helping African countries alleviate poverty and create sustainable economic growth had not materialized. Concerned world organizations such as the International Monetary Fund (IMF) and the World Bank offered to remedy Africa's situation to help them get out of the socio-economic and political crises, but under certain conditions. Thus, any country that sought help from the IMF and the World Bank had to agree to embark on reforms (economic, social, and political) which were/are expected to help the country in its socio-economic and political development.

Ghana was among the countries in Africa that was a model country for the successful implementation of the IMF-World Bank sponsored economic reforms and the Structural Adjustments Programmes. This even earned Ghana much admiration from other donors, with the effect that the country could easily get loans from many other sources too. Hence, Ghana went on a spree of taking loans from here and there. Many other African countries also succeeded in obtaining not only IMF-World Bank loans but also loans from other banks.

However, the expected results, such as alleviating mass poverty, creating jobs for the masses, and improving upon the general infrastructure have not been forthcoming, even well into the 21st century. In February 1990, an International Conference on Popular Participation in the Recovery and Development Process in Africa nearly declared war against the IMF and the World Bank-sponsored Structural Adjustments Programmes (SAP). At the conference in question, it was argued that the economic situation of any country in Africa that embarked on the implementation of the SAP had become worse than it was before receiving help from the foreign donors. However, a number of foreign donors, including the IMF and the World Bank, have always defended the good intentions of their help and the policies they suggest.

Over the years, I have pondered the legitimacy of asking for loans and/or help and the legitimacy of the donors to ask for some kind of guarantee for the efficient use of the loans or development help. One way to achieve the needed guarantee that loans and help would be used to achieve what they were intended for had been to impose some reforms. Unfortunately, many African countries have not been able to use the loans and development help as was expected of them. In the millennium many African countries, including Ghana, were so indebted that they had to apply again to the IMF, World Bank and several other donors for debt cancellation. To be given this relief, a country has had to apply and join the club of the Highly Indebted Poor Countries (HIPC) Initiative.

It appears that foreign loans and development help are a substitute for the indigenous resources (human and natural). To me, they are not. Rather, the foreign loans and development help are complementary to the indigenous resources and many countries have realized this. Several countries have, at some point in time, absorbed and used foreign aid and loans to alleviate mass poverty and improve upon the standards of living for their people. The Marshall Plan for European countries after World War II and the development help and loans to most Asian countries are a testimony to this complementary relationship between foreign loans, development help, and the indigenous resources. Therefore, by writing the "Development of a Country Is a Collective Effort: The Case of

Ghana", I have been inspired by the development efforts to alleviate poverty, create industrial capacity, acquire foreign inputs (loans and aid), breed entrepreneurship, and create enabling environments, which other countries have succeeded in doing. With experiences and/or lessons drawn from many sources, I am really inspired to write about the need for many actors in a society such as Ghana to be given the chance to contribute to the country's development. The development of a country is too huge a responsibility to be dominated by a single entity, the government or politicians or a few ruling elites.

Introduction

To begin, we highlight how Todaro (1994) sees development:

> "Development is the process of improving the quality of human lives. Three equally important aspects of development are (1) raising people's living levels – their incomes and consumption levels of food, medical services, education, etc., through relevant economic growth processes; (2) creating conditions conducive to the growth of people's self-esteem through the establishment of social, political, and economic systems and institutions that promote human dignity and respect; and (3) increasing people's freedom by enlarging the range of their choice variables, as by increasing varieties of consumer goods and services" (Todaro, 1994, p. 670).

Conventionally, a country's economic development is characterized by the development of its agricultural sector, followed by some basic manufacturing industries, which may process, for example, the produce from the agricultural sector; this is then followed by high-technology industries and services. But, with globalization touching every corner of the globe, many less developed countries may not have to go through the same pattern of development as many developed countries did. For example, markets, industries and governments are so interdependent that what happens in one corner of the globe can quickly be spread into others, thanks to advanced information technologies, transportation systems, and advanced educational systems. The challenge, however, will be the extent to which each and every country of the integrated world markets can prove to be competitive in relation to the competition it faces as firms from all over the world can enter any market, by a physical presence or by means of the Internet, Information Technologies (IT), and other communication technologies.

Globalization brings with it liberalization of markets, the dismantling of almost all trade barriers (Lee, 2005; Czinkota and Ronkainen, 2007). In Africa today, especially those south of the Sahara (including Ghana), foreign goods/services from foreign producers dominate in the markets. These goods and services may range from agriculturally processed goods (e.g. tin tomatoes from Europe) to sophisticated high-tech ones (e.g. computers, medical equipment, electronic equipment, mobile phones, cable T.V sets, and broadband services). The research and development and production centres of these goods and services are outside Africa. Africa is just a consuming market, where finished goods are brought and sold. The worst thing is that most countries that were self-sufficient, as far as satisfying their basic needs from agricultural products were concerned, are now very much reliant on what comes from abroad (Spiegel Special, 2007).

Indigenous firms in many African countries have been driven away from their markets because they could not match the competition from abroad. The globalization and its concomitant results, liberalization or market economies, have made it possible for many firms to serve several countries from their home markets (Czinkota and Ronkainen, 2007). The danger, which this development poses to many African countries, is the destruction of the industrial capacities of many African countries (Spiegel Special, 2007; Human Development Report, 2004). As will be seen later on in some of the chapters of this book, many infant industries that were established early in the 1960s by the Ghana government and private enterprises, have all fallen prey to the trade liberalization; they have been wiped away from the market.

Is trade liberalization a bad thing then, someone will ask? The answer is no. The forces of globalization and trade liberalization have enabled countries, firms, and private individuals to have a greater access to products and services. This in turn has increased people's freedom by enlarging the range of their choice variables by increasing varieties of consumer goods and services, as Todaro (1994, p. 670) might argue. However, to get a fair share of the competition in the integrated markets, countries, firms, and private individuals must be able to not only compete, but they also need to be able to make their exchange offers superior to those of competitors. And since markets need people with purchasing power, poverty alleviation, which will manifest itself in the rise of productivity and income of the masses in any society, is worth striving after. Ghana, our example, serves our purpose very well to highlight the phenomenon at issue, "development of a country is a collective effort".

In view of what has been discussed so far, we use Ghana's development efforts to highlight the need to involve many actors, which possess varied resources and perform heterogeneous activities in the society, in that endeavour. Where indigenous resources (human and natural) are inadequate, drawing on foreign inputs (e.g. loans and development help) should also be a crucial resource to consider. However, as will be seen in the following chapters, we stress that foreign inputs (loans and development help) should not be seen as a substitute for domestic resources, but rather they should be seen as complementary. The following quotation presents the incessant debate of some of the development paths Ghana should choose.

> "Indeed, despite efforts to alleviate poverty, Ghana still exhibits chronic inability to alleviate poverty. Many people still find it difficult to afford nutritious food, access to clean water and sanitation, energy, safe shelter, education and a healthy environment" (Development Debate, 2007)

In his lecture address at a Students' Forum at the Kwame Nkrumah University of Science and Technology (KNUST) in Kumasi last year, Professor Kwabena Frimpong-Boateng, Chief Executive Officer of the Korle-Bu Hospital Teaching Hospital, decried the inability of the nation to do things for itself as a result of the lack of a vibrant science and technology policy. He noted:

> "Building roads, construction of schools, hospitals, and digging boreholes with borrowed money or grants does not constitute development. Development, to me, is the process of developing the capacity to do things for

> ourselves and to be less and less dependent on foreign capital and technology." (Development Debate, 2007)

We will conclude this section by citing what an observer of Japan has to say about what developing countries can do.

> "I have spent much time on the Japanese experience for two reasons. First, it bore out what Harry Johnson said about the inadequacies of current policies on economic growth. Secondly, developing countries can learn from the slow and painful way the Japanese adapted their social and political institutions before growth through industrialisation became feasible. Developing countries today are in a more advantageous position than 19th century Japan in terms of the international involvement. What holds them back is not inadequate aid or trade, but their failure to establish competent organs of public administration and the failure to develop durable and enlightened social and political institutions" (Swee, 1995, p. 144).

The primary contribution of the present book lies in the systematic review of the incessant efforts made by Ghana, mostly development decisions being the sole prerogative of the ruling elites, showing what has been right and wrong and what needs be done to carve the way towards a sustainable development in Ghana. In all our discussions of the various themes in this book, we have adopted a business economist's perspective. This becomes obvious, as one reads the various chapters of this book. The rest of the book is structured as follows:

Chapter One: "Poverty Reduction is Beneficial for all Economic Agents." Here we emphasize the need to ensure that several actors in the society are given the chance to play a decisive role in the fight to reduce poverty.

Chapter Two: "The Historical Development of the Industrial Capacity of Ghana." Here we review the poor state of the industrial capacity during the colonial era and the attempts to build Ghana's industrial capacity during the post independent time.

Chapter Three: "Promoting Infant Industries in Less Developed Countries." Here we highlight the active involvement of the government in establishing basic industries in Ghana, as a way to lay the foundation for the country to become self-sufficient in possessing some basic industries; the successes and failures of this development and lessons thereof are also discussed.

Chapter Four: "The Search for Foreign Direct Investments (FDI)." This is about one of the foreign inputs which the country has been searching for over the years, with not much success. We discuss that, suggesting what can be done to increase the chances of getting more FDI.

Chapter Five: "Foreign Loans and Development Help in a Country's Economic Development." Here we highlight the importance of foreign inputs, but we advise on the efficient use of that. Efficient use of the foreign input will, among other things, be how the foreign inputs are seen and utilized as complementary resources to the indigenous resources.

Chapter Six: "The Need for Ghana to Encourage and Support Entrepreneurial Base Development." What is highlighted here is the relationship between the presence of effective entrepreneurial base and economic development. The opportunities and the difficulties which face Ghanaian entrepreneurs and how to help emerged entrepreneurs are also discussed.

Chapter Seven: "The Impact of Globalization and Liberalization of Trade." Here we discuss the opportunities and the challenges inherent in the increased integration and the dismantling of most trade barriers between nations.

Chapter Eight: "The Use of the Internet as a Marketing Strategy." Here we use three comparative case studies involving three companies, based in different countries, Brazil, Sweden, and Ghana, to highlight the effectiveness in using modern technology. This serves as a case to show how important it is for Ghanaian firms to adopt and use modern technologies, as the Ghanaian firm in the study has demonstrated.

Chapter Nine: "Collaborative Arrangements between Firms." In this chapter we discuss the need to have collaborative arrangements with other firms as a way of leveraging the partners' capabilities. Leveraging the partners' capabilities (in some collaborative arrangements) will enable them, among other things, match the intense competition and even serve the needs of their customers better than rivals can do.

Chapter Ten: "Carving the Way towards a Successful and Sustainable Development." In this concluding chapter, we sum up the discussions from Chapters One through Nine and add a few visionary suggestions for the future.

At the end of each chapter we provide references which have served as sources of our inspiration and also where the reader can read further on the theme addressed in the chapter. The **readership of this book** extends to students at universities, researchers/teachers, policy makers, especially in developing countries, Development Help Agencies the world over, business people, and politicians.

References

Czinkota, M.R., and Ronkainen, I. A. (2007). *International Marketing* (8 ed.), United States of America. Thomson South-Western.

Development Debate (2007). Debate on some development paths taken in Ghana, available at: http://www.ghanaweb.com/GhanaHomePage/NewsArchives/artikel.php?ID=119493: (Accessed, February 2, 2007).

Human Development Report (2004). By The United Nations Development Programme, New York , Oxford University Press.

Lee, K. (2005). *Global Marketing Management: Changes, Challenges, and New Strategies*, England. Oxford University Press.

Roe, A.R., (1991). *Economy.* In Regional Survey of the World: Africa South of Sahara (1992), 21st edition, Europe Publications Limited, London.

Swee, G.K., (1995). *Wealth of East Asian Nations*, Singapore Federal Publications Pte. Limited.

Todaro, M.P., (1994). *Economic Development*, 5th edition, Longman Publishing, New York.

World Development Report (1994). *Infrastructure for Development*. Published for the World Bank, Oxford/New York/Toronto, Oxford University Press.

World Development Report (1990). *Poverty,* Published for the World Bank, Oxford/new York/Toronto, Oxford University Press.

Contents

Abbreviations In The Book

ASEAN .... Association of South-East Asian Nations
CO_2 .... Carbon dioxide
CPI .... Corruption Perception Index
CRM .... Customer relationship management
DDHCH .... Doctor Den Hoed Clinic in Holland
ECOWAS .... Economic Community of West African States
ERP .... Economic Recovery Programme
EU .... European Union
FIAS .... Foreign Investment Advisory Service
FDI .... Foreign Direct Investment
HIPC .... Highly Indebted Poor Countries
HMC .... Hitachi Medical Corporation
GATT .... General Agreement on Tariffs and Trade
GPIC .... Ghana Investment Promotion Centre
IMF .... International Monetary Fund
ISSER .... Institute of Statistical and Economic Research
I.T .... Information Technology
JV .... Joint Venture
LDC .... Less Developed Countries
MNC .... Multinational Companies
NAFTA .... North American Free Trade Association
NIT .... New Information Technology
OPEC .... Organization of Petroleum Exporting Countries
PNDC .... Provisional National Defence Council
R&D .... Research and Development
SAP .... Structural Adjustment Programme
SMSC .... Scanditronix Medical Share Company
SSA .... Sub-Saharan Africa
TUC .... Trade Union Congress
VALCO .... Volta Aluminium Company
WTO .... World Trade Organization

Chapter One

Poverty Reduction Is Beneficial For All Economic Agents

Wearing the 'business glasses', we want to stress the important fact that the development of a nation is too big a task, with far-reaching effects, to be left to policy makers, here politicians, alone. In this book, therefore, we analyze Ghana's development efforts, highlighting the positive and the negative ones and suggesting some positive ways to carve the way toward a successful and sustainable development, which requires the participation of the actors depicted in Figure 1 below. The model below (Figure 1) serves as a starting point to bring into the picture other actors, who by interaction with governments, might also be given space to complement the efforts of governments (or policy makers) in the development of a nation.

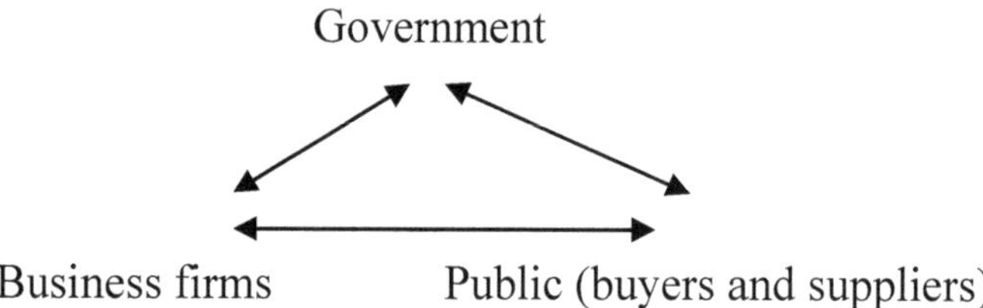

Figure 1: Interaction between Government, Businesses and the Public

Most governments stress the need to create welfare economies where the majority of the people are able to attain a minimal standard of living (World Development Report 1990). It is desirable for governments to provide and sustain the socio-economic well-being of all citizens in a particular country. This means to ensure that all have an acceptable minimum level of consumption (e.g. having nutritious food, access to clean water, energy, shelter, education, health facilities and enjoying protection of life and property). This minimum level of consumption, the so called poverty line, is the threshold to distinguish the poor from the non-poor (p. 27). There are country specific poverty lines and a universal poverty line, which permit cross-country comparison. For example, $275 and/or $370 per person a year was chosen to span the poverty lines estimated in recent studies for a number of countries with low average incomes (p. 27).

Nation Master's statistics of populations below poverty line by country presents some interesting reading. A few examples are provided below:

Countries	**Amount (top to bottom)**
Zambia	86%
Zimbabwe	80%
Chad	80%
Haiti	80%
Guatemala	75%
Suriname	70%
Paraguay	32%
Brazil	22%
Uruguay	22%
Egypt	20%
Israel	21%
United Kingdom	17%
Croatia	11%
Hungary	8.6%
France	6.5%
Belgium	4%
United States	12%
Canada	15.9%
Korea, South	15%
Malaysia	8%
Ghana	31.4%
Burkina Faso	45%
Nigeria	60%

Source: Nation Master, 2007

South Korea and Ghana are said to have had the same per capita income, $250, in the 1960s. Today, South Korea's per capita income is estimated to be over $5,000 while that of Ghana is about $300 (Development Debate, 2007). The number of people below the country's poverty line in Ghana is higher than that of South Korea as the above statistics show. However, we have to know that successive governments in Ghana have been trying to combat poverty.

Since its independence in 1957, Ghana's concern over the years has been to increase, among other things, productivity, employment opportunities, equitable distribution of income, per capita income and to guarantee security for life and property (Killick, 1981; Todaro; 1981; Ghana: Handbook of Commerce and Industry, 1988/89). However, 50 years after the country attained its independence, Ghana's per capita income is shown in the year 2007, to be hovering around $300 and should be a cause of concern.

What has gone wrong in the country's development efforts? Looking at the model above (Figure 1), interaction between government, businesses and the people, we can assign different roles and expectations to the various actors and discuss the need for them to complement each other in the effort to reduce poverty and increase productivity. Any attempt by only one actor to use its power to control and to dictate the exchange relationships between the three actors depicted in the model might result in the others either withdrawing from the exchange relationships or drastically reducing their cooperation and/or commitment. The actor, government, is not only responsible for making regulations and laws to promote the political, social and economic development of the country, it is also an active investor (taking the role of a business organization) in many sectors of the economy. For example, the Ghana government owns or is the majority owner in the electricity company, the railways, the water corporation and the Ghana Broadcasting Corporation.

The businesses or business firms in our model (the government might have shares in some of them) also have important roles to play in the development of the nation. Primarily, the businesses are in the marketplace to meet the various demands, which their various stakeholders (e.g. own workers, owners or shareholders, the government, customers, suppliers, trade unions and trade organizations) make on them (Awuah, 1994). The public, customers/consumers and suppliers, are the other actors that can also be in this category and may have needs, which may bring them into contact with businesses or the government, thereby establishing exchanges that create value and satisfaction for each of them. For instance, a practical illustration of the complementary efforts from the three actors depicted above will be to discuss the government's efforts to reduce poverty in the society and increase the general productivity in the society as well.

The correlation between poverty and productivity

Poverty, as argued by Harrison (1993), comes in two models, making it difficult to define the concept. All the same, Harrison attempts to define poverty based on each of the two models (absolute poverty and relative poverty).

Absolute poverty is defined as a level of income that imposes real physical suffering on people by hunger, disease and the massacre of innocent children. *Relative poverty*, on the other hand, is defined as the mental suffering that derives from inequality (Harrison, 1993, p. 418). The following illustrates these forms of poverty very well.

> "Even the poorest people in rich countries generally have much higher incomes than poor people in developing countries – but they still suffer severe deprivation. The reason? As a country gets richer, its inhabitants require more expensive goods and services to take part in normal life. Children may be unable to join in classroom conversations if their parents do not own a television; a construction worker may be unable to get work without a car. Such goods, once luxuries, become necessities as they proliferate throughout society. So, even in a rich country with no absolute income poverty, relative income poverty may lead to absolute poverty in important dimensions of human development – such as education, self-respect or the ability to get decent work" (Human Development Report, 2004, p. 20).

As defined in the World Development Report (1990, p. 26), poverty refers to the inability to attain a minimal standard of living. Common with the various definitions of poverty is that the poor lack the most essential needs of life. The other dimension of poverty, the relative poverty, as mentioned by Harrison (1993) is equally serious and needs be addressed. Inequality among a group of people may lead to envy, crime, sabotage, backbiting, and uncooperative behaviour. Hence, any effort to reduce poverty and increase productivity is worth the effort.

Studies have shown that improving the living conditions of the poor, through measures which are aimed at satisfying their basic needs, has a positive effect on their productivity (Todaro, 1989; Harrison, 1993; World Development Report, 1990). Most of the world's poor people live in rural areas in Less Developed Countries (LDC), where basic social amenities such as modern technologies, cheap and adequate credit facilities, efficient marketing systems, communication networks and good roads are lacking. Whether the people are engaged in farming or handicrafts, they are said to be shut off from the social amenities mentioned above (World Development Report, 1990: p1; p. 20). Any effort by a government in an LDC to provide its rural population access to the socio-economic amenities mentioned above will contribute to increasing their productivity and income. Where the poor also have access to such things as good sanitary conditions, better health care, adequate and nutritious food (i.e. enough calories, protein, vitamins and iron, for e.g.) their physical and mental capabilities and, for that matter, their productivity will be enhanced. Granting the poor people at least a full primary school education has also been found to be positively correlated with increased productivity of the poor (World Development Report, 1990).

As the income (i.e. the purchasing power) of the poor people increases, their general effective demand- i.e. ability to pay for what is demanded- (Armstrong, et al., 2005) for industrial goods (e.g. fertilizers, soaps, clothes and shoes) and services (provided both by the public and private businesses) may rise. Relating this positive relationship between poverty reduction and increased productivity to Ghana's example, the increase in demand from the masses may boost the production of the few manufacturing firms in the country, which face limited markets due to low demand (Awuah, 1997). In Ghana the poor outnumber the non-poor (Panford, 1994; Ghana Exporters' Directory, 1991, pp. 10-18). By the increased productivity of the masses, notably farmers, manufacturing firms processing agricultural products will reduce or stop imports of similar raw materials. Reducing poverty by taking the measures discussed here shows a multiplier effect which influences economic growth positively. In the model above (Fig. 1), the three actors, government, businesses and the general public will all have to be active, collaborate and create value together, which is sharable among them (Gummesson, 2002; Anderson and Narus, 2004). For example, the government, in the execution of its classic roles, should formulate and implement socio-economic policies that are in the best interest of the actors identified in the model.

The formulation and enforcement of monetary and fiscal policies should facilitate economic activities, and hence, enhance the exchange relationships between the actors. When policy instruments result in the opposite conditions (e.g. limited markets, low purchasing power of the masses, high inflation rate, lack of critical production inputs, and inefficient communication and transportation systems) manufacturing industries, among others, will be adversely affected. It has been reported that between 1975 and 1984 (Unicorn House Magazine, 1991, p. 3) some industries had to close their plants, very often due to lack of raw materials; the productivity of some industries, production per man hour, dropped by 75% because of lack of some critical raw materials, spare parts and the difficulty in obtaining government approval for certain imports. In the 1980s, the Ghanaian government recognized the underdevelopment of the rural areas. It therefore promised to improve the living conditions of the rural people by investing many resources in the development of the socio-economic infrastructure in the rural areas (Handbook of Commerce and Industry, 1988/89: 19). In the millennium, Ghana still has not been able to satisfactorily reduce poverty which might increase the productivity of the masses. A concerned Ghanaian quoted a fellow Ghanaian who has also expressed concern about Ghana's development:

> "Building roads, construction of schools, hospitals and digging boreholes with borrowed money or grants does not constitute development. Development, to me, is the process of developing the capacity to do things for ourselves and to be less and less dependent on foreign capital and technology.""Indeed, despite efforts to

alleviate poverty, Ghana still exhibits chronic inability to alleviate poverty. Many people still find it difficult to afford nutritious food and have access to clean water and sanitation, energy, safe shelter, education and a healthy environment" (Development Debate, 2007)

Interdependence among actors

The interdependence between the three actors in our model becomes very evident. Active interaction between them will enable them to address their common as well as their conflicting interests, seeking to enhance their common interests and reducing or eliminating the adverse effects of pursuing self-interests. Businesses are represented by people. A government is represented by people. The public, which is here seen to compose of buyers and sellers, are also represented by people. Shouldn't there be a way to have some representatives of the three actors regularly interact to exchange ideas, knowledge and information regarding how the parties will together create value (something which none of them acting alone can do), thereby meeting the needs of the actors and the people they represent? The regular interaction, relationships, and exchanges between the actors (their representatives) in Ghana seems to be non-existent or not functioning as they should be

All nations that have made some major strides in their development have what we call 'think tanks' (Parsons, 1995) that are built using actors such as those identified in the model above. 'Think tanks' are given the task to identify opportunities and problems which might enhance or deter the development and sustenance of exchange relationships among economic actors in a nation. 'Think tanks' build scenarios regarding the changes, some occur gradually and others very suddenly, that are going on within a nation and within the world at large. The 'think tanks' are giving the freedom and the resources to think out how to exploit the windows of opportunities which are likely to emerge from the changes. They are also to think out solutions to threats that can emanate from the changes or suggest warning systems that will help avoid threats. The members in a 'think tank' are obliged to report and consult with the people they represent so that ideas, knowledge and information of importance will be exchanged and acted upon. Ghana needs to develop this 'facilitating' organ of 'think tanks' which might enhance the exchange relationships between the actors in our model (Fig. 1).

Besides building 'think tanks', Ghana can also learn from the experiences of other countries that have embarked on effective programmes to combat poverty, which have helped them to build simultaneously healthy economies. Indonesia and Malaysia, for example, are cited as countries that, since the 1960s, have been balancing regional development and reducing poverty respectively. These countries are said to have achieved the above objectives by directing infrastructure expenditures, especially in transport and irrigation, to rural areas. Malaysia's rural poverty, which in 1973 affected 53.3 percent of the population, fell to 19.3 percent in 1989, as reported in the World Development Report (1990: 80). Malaysia has only 8 % of her population below the poverty line, as reported in the above Nation Master's statistics. A country's ability to reduce poverty, as the examples of Indonesia and Malaysia show, will in large measure, require massive general investments (from both government and private investors) and improved social services that may benefit all economic agents.

In Ghana the dominant occupation in the rural areas is agriculture, most people living on subsistence farming (Ghana: handbook of Commerce and Industry, 1988/89). The people in the rural areas are not only using out-dated techniques in farming, but most of them have no access to irrigation systems, high-yield seeds or crops with short mature life, and cheap and adequate credit facilities. As the result of that, their productivity is very low. Their income is also very low, limiting their ability to effectively satisfy most essential needs. As a result of the low income and productivity of the masses, businesses are also faced with limited markets in Ghana (Awuah, 1994; Roe, 1991). The following quotation describes the situation of a typical rural family in Ghana.

> "In Ghana's savannah region a typical family of seven lives in three one-room huts made of mud bricks, with earthen floors. They have little furniture and no toilet, electricity, or running water…

> ...The family has few possessions, apart from three acres of unirrigated land and one cow, and virtually no savings" (World Development Report, 1990: 24).

Attempts to combat poverty

Attempts to combat poverty in the rural areas in Ghana, when successful, might lead to increase productivity and income of the people, but Ghana's policy makers have in the past neglected the importance of involving many other interest groups in that development effort (Panford, 1994; Tangari, 1992; World Development Report, 1994: 48). For any development programme to be successful, the services users need to be involved in the formulation and implementation of any development project (World Development Report, 1994: 48). Ghana has not scored well on this count. As reported in Akwetey (1994, p. p. 86), there was a time that the leadership of the Trade Union Congress (TUC) had to criticize PNDC for the arbitrary manner in which it took decisions that affected the interest of labour without any prior consultations or discussions. But, as illustrated in our model above, actors that are interdependent would have to eschew unilateral action, for the sake of "win-win" and long-run exchange relationships. The development of a nation is too big a task to be relegated to only policy makers.

Summary

In summary, the Ghanaian development problems, when using the "business glasses", suggest that the three actors identified in our model (see Fig. 1) ought to have active roles in bringing about exchange relationships, which will enable the government to achieve its goal of creating a welfare state, where the masses will have jobs, increased income and access to socio-economic infrastructures that will facilitate their productivity. Channelling most of the resources gained from the cancellation of Ghana's 7 billion dollars debt to areas of social services and infrastructure in order to improve the lives of the people, a declaration made by the incumbent president on February 24, 2007, is in the right direction and needs be supported.

Businesses stand to gain when the masses have the ability to demand and pay for goods and services they need. Businesses also gain when suppliers to the business companies are able to supply adequate and qualitative production inputs. Business companies gain when the government's monetary and fiscal policies are not detrimental but congenial to the conduct of business in the enabling environment. Where businesses thrive and grow, they create jobs, pay taxes and engage in supporting or sponsoring social investments in such areas as education, health, environmental protection and community work. With the masses having increased income to consume, invest and pay taxes, the government stands to gain by having a substantial tax base, from which further socio-economic infrastructure can be developed. Businesses will also benefit from a large number of the population that have increased income (i.e. purchasing power). Effective demand of goods and services might emerge. This brings us to look closely into the historical development of the industrial capacity of Ghana in Chapter Two.

References

Akwetey, E. (1994). *Trade Unions and Democratization: A Comprehensive Study of Zambia and Ghana*, Dissertation, Department of Political Science, University of Stockholm, Stockholm.

Anderson, J.C & Narus, J.A. (2004). *Business Market Management: Understanding, Creating and Delivering Value* (2nd ed.), New Jersey: Pearson Education, Inc.

Armostrong, G., Kotler, P., Saunders, J & Wong, V. (2005). *Principles of Marketing* (4th Ed.); Harlow: Person Education Limited.

Awuah, G. B. (1994). *The Presence of Multinational Companies (MNCs) in Ghana: A Study of the Interaction between an MNC and Three Indigenous Firms*, Dissertation, Department of Business Studies, Uppsala University, Uppsala.

Awuah, G. B. (1997). Promoting Infant Industries in Less Developed Countries (LDC): A Network Approach to Analyze the Impact of the Exchange Relationships between Multinational Companies and their Indigenous Suppliers in LDC's Effort to Boost Infant Industries' Development. *International Business Review*, 6 (1), 71-87.

Development Debate (2007). Debate on some development paths taken in Ghana, available at: http://www.ghanaweb.com/GhanaHomePage/NewsArchives/artikel.php?ID=119493: (Accessed, February 2, 2007)

Ghana Exporters' Directory. (1991). *World Wide Press Ltd.*, Accra.

Ghana: *Handbook of Commerce and Industry*, (1988/89). Ministry of Trade and Tourism, Accra.

Gummesson, E. (2002). *Total Relationship Marketing: Marketing Management, Relationship Strategy and CRM Approaches for the Network Economy* (2nd Ed.); Oxford: Butterworth Heinemann.

Harrison, P. (1993). *Inside the Third World: The Anatomy of Poverty* (3rd Ed.) Middlesex, England Penguin Book Ltd.

Human Development Report (2004). By The United Nations Development Programme, New York , Oxford University Press.

Killick, T. (1981). *Policy Economics: A Textbook of Applied Economics on Developing Countries*. London, Heinemann.

Nation Master (2007). Nation Master's Statistics of Population below the Poverty Line. Available at: http://www.nationmaster.com: (accessed 27-03-2007).

Panford, K. (1994). Structural Adjustment, the State and Workers in Ghana: An African Development, *Quarterly Journal of the Council for the Development of Social Science Research*, Codesria, Dakar.

Parsons, W. (1995). *Public Policy: An Introduction to the Theory and Practice of Policy Analysis*, Cheltenham, Edward Elgar Publishing Limited.

Roe, A.R. (1991). *Economy*. In Regional Survey of the World: Africa South of Sahara (1992), (21st ed.). London, Europe Publications Limited.

Tangari, R. (1992). The Politics of Government – business relations in Ghana. The *Journal of Modern African Studies* 30, 97-111.

World Development Report (1994). *Infrastructure for Development.* Published for the World Bank, Oxford/New York/Toronto, Oxford University Press.

World Development Report (1990). *Poverty,* Published for the World Bank, Oxford/New York/Toronto, Oxford University Press.

Chapter Two

The Historical Development Of The Industrial Capacity Of Ghana

The colonial remnants

As reported elsewhere (Shaw, 1973, p. 14), the poor state of the entrepreneurial base and the comparatively primitive domestic markets, especially the finance, in many less developing countries (LDC) are blamed on the colonial administrators' sheer negligence of the economic development of the majority of the countries that once had colonial governments. The colonial governments are said to have also given biased support to only multinational companies (MNC), which operated at the time in the colonies (Mckinon, 1973, pp. 69-70). Local entrepreneurial capacity development was not encouraged. Most African countries, including Ghana, were victims of the type of industrial development which the colonial governments built in their territories. As reported in the Spiegel Special (2007:31), the colonial rulers in Africa left behind underdeveloped states; the African politicians are said to have inherited a house without foundation.

Hence, most African countries, after attaining independence, saw a remedy in the governments′ direct intervention in their economic systems (Shaw, 1973). A government's direct intervention could manifest itself in many spheres. For instance, in the interest of society, a government could control general prices, foreign exchange, and restrict some imports of foreign goods and services. Some private firms, mostly MNCs operating during the colonial era, were nationalised. The government also actively invested in the economy, resulting in the establishment of a number of state enterprises.

Many LDC governments aimed at achieving economic self- sufficiency. The colonial administrators left many LDCs to be dependent on only one-sided economies (Killick, 1981; Todaro, 1981), exporting mainly raw materials to the developed world. In this regard, many MNCs that operated during the colonial era were looked upon as agents of exploitation and therefore needed be gotten rid of. The following illustrates this point:

> "FDI may result in foreign control of the national economy. Ownership of natural resources such as oil and natural gas, coal or mineral deposits by foreigners may mean that these non-renewable assets are exploited for the short-term gain of the foreigners, not in the long-term benefit of the host country's citizens" (Griffin, R., et al, 1998, p.133).

Achieving self-sufficiency

The imposition of numerous trade restrictions, nationalisation of some private MNCs and control of financial institutions were all explanations for achieving economic self- sufficiency (Hymer, 1975; Kirkpatrick et al., 1983; Todaro, 1981, 1989; Killick, 1981). Ghana's incessant efforts to build its own industrial capacity were, therefore, to be seen in the country's strive to achieve self-sufficiency. Ghana needed to broaden its industrial base because its reliance on traditional exports products (e.g. gold, diamond, bauxite, and manganese) was a cause of concern (Ghana Exporters' Directory, 1991; Roe, 1991). Ghana's heavy dependence on primary products was a great concern for policy makers right after the country's attainment of independence, so government's direct intervention to effect desirable economic development became commonplace. A typical example was when the government of Ghana, as a means to restrict imports of certain commodities, asked foreign producers of those goods to come into the country to set up local production (Todaro, 1989, p. 435; Fieldhouse, 1978, p. 412).

As reported in Fieldhouse (1978, p. 412), the economic climate in Ghana had already deteriorated by the 1960s. The country suffered from an accelerated adverse balance of trade, something that was attributed to reduced cocoa prices and to government spending. It was therefore important to wean the country from the importing of goods and services (see Chapter Three). Instead, foreign producers were encouraged to come and do local production (Fieldhouse, 1978). Failure to come and undertake local production would mean that the foreign producer would no longer be allowed to export to Ghana (Fieldhouse, 1978). Fieldhouse reports Unilever's experience in Ghana, as the then government massively intervened in the economy:

> "It was perfectly happy with an export market that provided as much as £150,000 pre-tax profits in the 1950s and there is no indication in the records of hope that local production would provide a better return. But by the later 1950s the concern was faced with a stark choice: invest or probably lose an established import market to whichever enterprise, public or private, was allowed to set up the one large soap factory that Ghana market could support" (Fieldhouse, 1978, pp. 416-417).

Intervention as a means to accelerate the building of industrial capacity

In the words of Okoso-Amaa (1975, p. 11), intervention can be defined as a process whereby a government can take certain timely actions in the market to help or coerce some of the interest groups in such a way that more desirable results in business or in terms of the system's performance can be achieved. Successive Ghana governments have intervened in the economic development processes with varied results. The efforts exerted so far to build the local industrial capacity needs to be critically examined. The need to embark on the internal industrial capacity building has been going on in Ghana since the 1950s (Garlick, 1971; Ghana Hanbook of Commerce and Industry, 1988). During the era of Prime Minister Dr. Kwame Nkrumah, for example, Ghana's efforts to build the industrial capacity was vehemently promoted on the development agenda. The then Prime Minister was said to have declared:

> "I wish to emphasize that the government is determined to expand the industrial capacity of Ghana, and that private capital and technical know-how are welcome from any source, whether from within or from outside Ghana" (Garlick, 1971, p. 119).

The Prime Minister went on to promise foreign investors incentives and protection of their property.

> "Although he believed in state socialism, he also accepted that rapid development in the consumer goods sector depended on direct foreign investment, and he seemed willing to attract such investment by providing tariff protection, tax concessions in the early years, guarantee for the safety of foreign property and state action to provide essential services" (Fieldhouse 1978, pp. 412-413)

Admittedly, foreign direct investors were expected to come to Ghana to invest and contribute to the building of the industrial capacity of the nation. As reported elsewhere (Harrison, 1993, p. 357), 50% of the 1974 manufacturing sales in Ghana were accounted for by foreign-owned enterprises. Succeeding governments in Ghana have also continued to attract foreign direct investors into the country. In Chapter Four, we will look critically at Ghana's effort to attract foreign direct investment.

Ghana's Investment Code, PNDC Law 116, defines large areas that are intended for private investment, the incentives and guarantees to investors, both foreign and Ghanaians (Ghana: Handbook of Commerce and Industry, 1988; Financial Times, July 11, 1989: 3). Bilateral and multilateral protection agreements have been signed which should assure the safety of investors' property while operating in Ghana (Financial Times, 1989: 3, Asante et al., 2000). But somewhere along the way, succeeding governments have failed to be consistent and trustworthy with their promises to the business community.

Paradoxically enough, various governments in Ghana have intervened massively in the economy so that private investors have had less freedom of action to conduct their businesses.

"Many African and foreign businessmen felt in 1960-62, during the survey, that their position was made insecure by government policy. Import licensing, tight exchange control (both of which to a large extent reflected economic difficulties stemming from the sharp fall in cocoa prices), and government plans to undertake importing, wholesaling, and retail 'co-operative' trading seemed to foreshadow a discouraging future for private enterprise of any size" (Garlick, 1971, p. 122).

The efforts to encourage private investors to contribute towards the industrial capacity building in Ghana, as the above quote portrays, was already stifled by the 1960s (Roe, 1991). Much of the 1970s too bore witness to the state intervention in the economic activities of private investors (Roe, 1991; Panford, 1994; Tangari, 1992). For Panford (1994), political factors played a role in Ghana to scare away investors, both active and potential ones. Too much state intervention in the activities of private firms did destroy the investment climate. And the State was also accused of harassing businessmen (Tangari, 1992, pp. 100-101). Investors lost confidence in Ghana (Tangari, 1992; Asante et al., 2000; Kuada and Sorensen, 2001). The above scenarios and the several control mechanisms (price, import, foreign exchange and interest rate controls) which were in place during most parts of the 1960s and 1970s produced the effect that firms' freedom of action became summarily restricted. (Roe, 1991; Business and Financial Times, October 30- November 12, 1991: 4) All this led to the fact that the manufacturing sector's output stagnated in the 1970s and then declined in the early 1980s (Roe, 1991). Consequently, the manufacturing sector's contribution to Ghana's GDP fell from 22% in 1973 to under 5% before the start of the government's economic reforms in 1983 (p. 512).

Government interventions and negative economic policies also impacted the production of cocoa, especially in the 1970s (Roe, 1991), and the mining sector. Several mines became unprofitable so they closed down (Ghana Exporters' Directory, 1991, p. 15). It has been reported that Ghana had 30 gold mines in 1936; but by 1983, the total number of gold mines in Ghana was only four (p. 15). Realizing that massive intervention (control mechanisms imposed in several sectors, nationalization of some private businesses and harassment of businesspeople) could not improve Ghana's effort to build her industrial capacity, the severe economic crisis that emanated forced a change of direction. This is in line with what has been observed elsewhere.

"The early literature on growth saw economic transformation of poor countries in terms of building what was termed "the modern sector". This centred on the growth of the manufacturing industry through producing goods that were formerly imported. Since the free market mechanism would not produce the transformation, government intervention through a series of five-year plans was necessary. In practice, this required the imposition of "shut-out" tariffs, licensing of industries, exchange controls and import licensing. It is now evident that this strategy did not work" (Swee, G.K, 1995, p. 127)

In 1983, the government in power in Ghana launched an Economic Recovery Programme as a means to address the negative impacts of government interventions in the economy. Among other things, most controls (e.g. price, interest rate, foreign exchange and import) had to be abolished. Trade liberalization and reformation of the legal framework to safeguard and/or protect individuals and their business property were also undertaken. All this was expected to create a favourable business climate for investors, facilitate economic growth and thereby enhance the living standard of the people of Ghana (Roe, 1992; Ghana: Handbook of Commerce and Industry; 1988/89; World Development Report, 1994).

Some positive effects of the economic reforms were manifested in the performance of the manufacturing sector, which had suffered during the era of massive intervention and control. For instance, in 1986, the manufacturing sector's contribution to GDP came close to 10%. This was an improvement that was attributed to the liberalization policies and the government's active investment to improve the socio-economic infrastructure (Roe, 1991, p. 512; Ghana: Handbook of Commerce and Industry, 1988). The government, through the reform, was said to have won admiration from outside and also inspired confidence in the country (Roe, 1991; Africa Economic Digest, Vol. II, No. 3, January 22-28, 1990:3). Because of the reforms, Ghana gained access to foreign institutions such as the International Monetary Fund (IMF), the World Bank and other banks. For the World Bank, Ghana became, after China and India, its greatest recipient of interest free development loans (Svenska Dagbladet, January 18, 1989:4; Der Spiegel 35/1989:142).

Reforms that were not perceived as genuine

The positive effects of the reforms were not sustainable because there was a lack of policies and programmes to ensure that many people, in general, and businesses, in particular, were involved in the process of reform and hence benefited from it. A range of criticisms were levelled against the little consideration which the government took about Ghana's transformation capacity (Panford, 1994; Tangari, 1992). Among other things, the government was accused of not having the administrative ability to implement reforms, which had severe effects on the majority of the people, particularly the urban and the rural poor. The success of the reforms, as was recorded, were said to be the result of the government's sole concentration on bringing the general excessive demand in the economy to some manageable level. The problems of the poor were left untouched. The mass lay-off of workers from the public sector, removal of almost all government subsidies, and the introduction of cost recovery system – where the consumption of social services such as electricity, health care, and education were to be paid in full – had a severe blow on many households (Panford, 1994, pp. 80-86). Some consequences of the restrictive reforms were the increased illiteracy and drop-out rates, malnutrition, illness, and unsanitary conditions in many areas of the urban towns (Ghana Today, June, 1994: 17-24; Chronicle, May 1993: 10).

The absorption capacity of the few manufacturing firms that were expected to absorb the large number of people thrown out of jobs in the public sector was very low or weak. Many workers were also thrown out of jobs from the manufacturing sector because many businesses had to close. Firms that could not face competition when trade in Ghana was liberalized had to close down, thereby rendering many workers jobless (Tangari, 1992, p. 101). The net effect was that the low general purchasing power of the masses and the general liquidity problems facing domestic producers played a role to limit the manufacturing firms' abilities to expand and create jobs. The government was unable to deal with the fact that Ghana was a heterogeneous society, with many interest groups such as urban workers, professionals, industrialists, students, traders, farmers, and the poor (both in urban and rural areas). As the critics pointed out, no reform will materialize, in the long run, without involving the various groups in the formulation and implementation of it (Panford, 1994, p. 86; Tangari, 1992). As reported in the World Development Report (1994: 48), development programmes are more successful when service users or the affected community has been involved in project formulation and implementation. But in Ghana, Tangari (1992) had this to report:

> "The general negative reaction of the P.N.D.C to the plight of the indigenous enterprises brought it into sharp conflict with sections of the business community" (Tangari, 1992, p. 102).

In comparing Ghana's development to that of South Korea's (Human Development Report, 2004), external observers also added their voice to the dominance of the government of Ghana in the economy and the exclusion of many interests groups, especially the business community.

In the introductory essay, "Culture Count", Huntington writes:

> "In the early 1990s, I happened to come across economic data on Ghana and South Korea in the early 1960, and I was astonished to see how similar their economies were then… Thirty years later, South Korea had become an industrial giant with the fourteenth largest economy in the world, multinational corporations, major exports of automobiles, electronic equipment, and other sophisticated manufactures, and per capita income approximately that of Greece. Moreover it was on its way to the consolidation of democratic institutions. No such changes had occurred in Ghana, whose per capita income was about one-fifteenth that of South Korea's. How could this extraordinary difference in development be explained? Undoubtedly, many factors played a role, but it seemed to me that culture had to be a large part of the explanation. South Koreans valued thrift, investment, hard work, education, organization, and discipline. Ghana had different values. In short, cultures count.
>
> "…There may well be something of interest in this engaging comparison (perhaps even a quarter- truth torn out of context), and the contrast does call for probing

> examination. But the causal story is extremely deceptive. There were many important differences – other than cultural predispositions – between Ghana and the Republic of Korea in the 1960s, when the countries appeared to Huntington to be much the same, except for culture. The class structures in the two countries were quite different, with a much larger role of business classes in Korea. The politics were very different too, with the government in Korea eager to play a prime-moving role in initiating business-centred economic development in a way that did not apply in Ghana. The close relationship between the Korean economy and the Japanese and US economies also made a big difference, at least in the early stages of Korean development. Perhaps most important, by the 1960s Korea had a much higher literacy rate and a more extensive school system than Ghana had. The Korean changes had been brought about largely through resolute public policy since the Second World War, and were not simply a reflection of age-old Korean culture" (Human Report, 2002, p. 19)

Evidently, the reader might gain some insights from the above quotes from the Human Development Report (2004), comparing Ghana with South Korea as both embarked on building their respective industrial capacities, regarding factors that are of crucial importance to industrial capacity of a nation. Without much information on South Korea, because it is beyond the scope of this book, Ghana's achievement from the various interventions needs be stated here. Ghana's outcomes from her nationalizations and interventions during most of the 1960s and 1970s (Asante et al., 2000; Panford, 1994; Tangari, 1992; Roe, 1991; Todaro, 1989; Kilick, 1981) did not only destroy the investment climate of Ghana, but also scared away investors from Ghana. South Korea, with a more business friendly climate and better relationships with economic giants such as the US and Japan, coupled with resolute public policy (Human Development Report, 2004), is apparently better off in terms of industrial capacity building. The challenge, which Ghana needs to handle, will be to have the ability and the political will to promote cooperation among the government and all interested groups in the society. This will, among other things, facilitate the identification of the most vulnerable groups and the means by which they can be helped.

From the general development and the industrial capacity building point of view, vulnerable groups can be: the poor in the society, firms that are not able to compete because of intense competition with foreign goods and services, and almost all the rural people who lack access to modern infrastructure which will integrate the economic activities of the rural people with those of the urban areas.

"The under-developed socio-economic infrastructure may well explain the paucity of manufacturing industries in the rural areas. If a firm is to reach such people it must possess the means and the expertise to extend its activities to wide areas of the countryside. The low income of the rural folk inhibits demand. Many have to be reached, if penetration into the rural areas is to be worth the effort, for the cost involved in coming into contact with as many as possible can be very high. This also explains why many firms face a limited market in the country" (Awuah, 1994, p. 45).

Capacity building: an effort by many actors

It has to be kept in mind that development efforts and industrial capacity building efforts should embody the realization that specific actors (individuals, organisations, and firms), controlling specific resources, and performing specific activities (Håkansson and Snehota, 1995) are to be involved in the process. Actors involved in the process of industrial capacity building and how they relate to each other and the linkage effect (Caves, 1982) of their interdependence need be identified and promoted so that efficient and effective contributions will be made in the filling of the 'input-output table' (to borrow Caves's term) of the country, which has been empty for too long. For Caves (p. 271), encouraging a specific demand for an output, or a concrete supply of an input, may provoke a viable activity. This is because a firm's behaviour, its performance and/or creation of linkages are influenced by its exchange relationships with certain other actors (e.g. other businesses, government, organisations, and private individuals) in a network of exchange relationships. Chapter Three illustrates this phenomenon by closely analyzing the role business firms (both public and private owned) can play in Ghana's effort to develop its industrial capacity and discusses efforts to develop and sustain import-substitution industries or infant industries.

Current trend in government policies

Ghana is a regime which is no longer perceived as a controlled economy. It is liberalised and the relationship between businesses and the government seems not to be that of antagonism but that of harmony. A recent report on the economic climate in Ghana is worth reporting:

> "While Ghana is a low-income country, it was considered 'relatively well-managed' with good prospects for economic growth. A World Bank study in 1996 found deficiencies in the procurement framework but on that issue, as many other policy areas, the country was commended for moving in the right direction. The business environment had been liberalized and IVO staff described Ghana as easy to work in. The bureaucracy was described as 'serious' and 'efficient', and the authorities were helpful in solving problems encountered by the project staff" (Owusu and Welch, 2007, p. 152).

The above quotation is an indication that the cooperation agitated for in this book between the government and all interests groups in the society, as the country embarks on building its industrial capacity, is emerging in Ghana. Instead of the authorities harassing businesspeople, as some previous regimes in Ghana allowed, here we have authorities being described as helpful. All the same, on the economic growth side, Ghana has a long way to go; this will demand intensive and extensive cooperation among the actors identified in this chapter.

> "There is no denying the fact that Ghana is endowed with unique natural and human resources that could significantly contribute to the quality of life and economic prosperity of the citizenry. However, there are constraints in mobilising, allocating and utilising these resources to achieve higher per capita income levels and thereby help to reduce poverty at the individual level and at the national level as well.
>
> "... The most significant of these challenges is the failure to formulate a comprehensive and coherent national

science and technology policy designed to contribute to the achievement of the country's development objectives.

> "...Even though, our society depends on science and technology for its survival, successive governments had failed to realise this, a development that had resulted in a situation where Ghana even after 50 years of independence still import almost everything and produces virtually nothing"(Development Debate, 2007).

The above quotation also points to the fact that the reforms in place (World Development Report, 1994; Roe, 1991; Ghana Exporters' Directory, 1991; Asante et al, 2000; Ghana: Handbook of Commerce and Industry, 1988/89) which put Ghana on the right and desirable direction, might facilitate the identification and the investment in areas that have the potential to help achieve the country's goals. Hence, many interest groups such as institutions, urban workers, professionals, industrialists, students, traders, farmers, and the poor (both in urban and rural areas), should be involved in the transformation process. The building of an industrial capacity that would be sustainable over a very long period of time would demand that cooperation.

Summary

In summary, Ghana, like many LDCs, has had the reason to seriously invest in the building of its industrial capacity because the colonial administrators neglected the economic development of the country (Shaw, 1973; Killick, 1981; Todaro, 1989), leaving behind a weak entrepreneurial base and the comparatively primitive domestic markets. Indeed, various governments in Ghana have made efforts to build the industrial capacity of the country with varied results. Although public and private investments were considered equally important for the development of the industrial capacity of the country, unfortunately, private investments were subjected to massive restrictions. Nationalisations of private businesses became commonplace. State interventions, which prevented private businesspeople from having freedom of action produced not only a hostile investment climate, but investors (both foreign and nationals) were scared away from investing in Ghana. In the 1980s, the deterioration of the economy was exacerbated so much so that the policy makers in the country were compelled to undertake genuine economic reforms that were hoped would transform the economy, one that would meet the expectations of all.

Trade liberalisation, removal of most controls that have stifled businesses, resolute and/or sound policies that would enable the government to provide favourable conditions, which other actors (e.g. ordinary private individuals, business firms and organisations) cannot create themselves, and interaction between the government and several interest groups would go a long way to facilitate the exchange relationships between the actors. Since the actors are, more or less, interdependent, cooperation between them should be emphasised.

References

African Digest, Vol. 11, No. 3, January 22-28, 1990:3.

Akwetey, E. (1994). *Trade Unions and Democratization: A Comprehensive Study of Zambia and Ghana*, Dissertation, Department of Political Science, University of Stockholm, Stockholm.

Asante, Y., Gyasi, E.M., and Tsikata, G.K (2000). *Determinants of Foreign Direct Investment in Ghana*, Overseas Development Institute, Portland House, Stage Place, London SW1E 5DP.

Asiedu, E. (2001). On the Determinants of Foreign Direct Investment to Developing Countries: Is Africa Different? *World Development* Vol. 30, No. 1, pp. 107-119.

Awuah, G. B. (1994). *The Presence of Multinational Companies (MNCs) in Ghana: A Study of the Interaction between an MNC and Three Indigenous Firms*, Dissertation, Department of Business Studies, Uppsala University, Uppsala.

Business and Financial Times, October 30 – November 12, 1991:4.

Caves, R.E., (1982), *Multinational Enterprise and Economic Analysis*, Cambridge Press University.

Chronicle, May, 1993: 10

Der Spiegel 35/1989:142

Development Debate (2007), Debate on some development paths taken in Ghana, available at: http://www.ghanaweb.com/GhanaHomePage/NewsArchives/artikel.php?ID=119493: (Accessed, February 2, 2007)

FIAS (2003). *Ghana: Administrative Barriers to Investment Update*, Accra.

Fieldhouse, D.K. (1978). *"Unilever Overseas" – The Anatomy of a Multinational*, 1895-1965, London , Croom-Helm.

Financial Times, July 11, 1989:3

Ghana Today, June 1994: 17-24

Garlick, P.C., (1971). *African Traders and Economic Development in Ghana*, Clarendon Press, Oxford, London.

Griffin, R., Mahoney, D., Pustay, M., Trigg, M, (1998). *International Business*, Longman, South Melbourne, Australia.

Human Development Report (2004). By The United Nations Development Programme, New York , Oxford University Press.

Hymer, S. (1975). "The Multinational Corporation and the Law of Uneven Development" In: Lundgren, N., De internationella koncernena och samhällsekonomi, Tiden Barnägen trykerier, pp. 228-258 (1970/75).

Håkansson, H., and Snehota, I. (1995). *Developing Relationships in Business Networks*. London: Routledge.

Kirkpatrick, C:P, Lee, N., & Nixson, F.I. (1983). *Industrial Structure and Policy in Less Developed Countries*, London: Heinemann.

Kuada, J and Sorensen, O.J., (2001). Firms in the South: Interactions between National Business Systems and the Global Economy. In: Jakobsen, G and Torp, J.E (Editors), *Understanding Business Systems in Developing Countries*, Sage Publications, New Delhi/London.

McKinnon, R. I (1973). *Money and Capital in Economic Development*, Washington Brookings Institution.

Okoso-Amaa, K. (1975). *Rice Marketing in Ghana: An Analysis of Government Interventions in Business*. Scandinavia Institute of African Studies, Uppsala.

Owusu, R.A, and Welch, C. (2007). The Buying Network in International Project Business: A Comparative Case Study of Development Projects, *Industrial Marketing Management* 36, pp. 147-157.

Shaw, E. S. (1973). *Financial Deepening in Economic Development*, London.
Spiegel Special Geschichte (2007) Nr. 2, 22-05-07: 31
Svenska Dagbladet, January 18, 1989:4
Swee, G.K., (1995). *Wealth of East Asian Nations*, Singapore Federal Publications Pte. Limited.

Chapter Three

Promoting infant industries in Less Developed Countries (LDC): a network approach to analyse the impact of the exchange relationships between multinational companies and their indigenous suppliers in LDCs' efforts to boost infant industries' development*

Promoting Infant Industries in Less Developed Countries (LDCs): a 'Network Approach to Analyse the Impact of the Exchange Relationships between Multinational Companies and their Indigenous Suppliers in LDCs' Efforts to Boost Infant Industries' Development

Gabriel B. Awuah

University of Skövde, Department of Business Administration, Economics and Statistics, PO Box 408, S-541 28 Skövde, Sweden

Abstract - Promoting domestic production of certain goods/services has always been spurred by, e.g. a country's need to create job opportunities,

---

* This article was published in the International Business Review, Volume 6, Number 1, "Promoting Infant Industries in Less Developed Countries (LDCs): A Network Approach to Analyse the Impact of the Exchange Relationships between Multinational Companies and Their Indigenous Suppliers in LDCs' Efforts to Boost Infant Industries' Development" , pp. 71-87, Copyright Elsevier, 1997. Permission has been granted by Elsevier for the reproduction of this article.

to generate internal sources of revenue for general development, and to wean the country from its dependence on imports of goods/services which may not only exacerbate its terms of trade with other countries, but also inhibit the achievement of the other objectives mentioned above. LDCs' efforts to promote infant industries have wide coverage in the literature, yet little attention has been paid to the role certain specific actors, controlling specific resources and performing specific activities play in the success of such a developmental process. Drawing on the industrial network approach, this article seeks to deepen our understanding of the impact of the exchange relationships between multinational companies and their indigenous suppliers in the process of promoting infant industries in LDCs.

Key Words - Infant Industries, Network, Exchange Relationships, Multinational Companies, Indigenous Suppliers, Import-substitution, Learning, Competence, Regulation, Deregulation

Introduction

The promotion of infant industries by any country is not a new phenomenon (cf. Södersten, 1970; Timmermann, 1982). However, the method employed to foster the development of infant industries may differ from country to country. All the same, there seems to be a common denominator on which all efforts to encourage the sustainable development and/or survival of infant industries, once started, can be reduced. Thus, almost all countries try to impose restrictions on imports of certain goods/services in order to protect certain domestic industries which, by so doing, also leads to the protection of incomes and jobs at home (cf. Killick, 1981; Unger, 1988; Economist, 1994b: p.22).

Throughout the 1960s and the 1970s many LDCs, for e.g. implemented import-substitution (IS) strategies as a measure to promote infant industries (cf. Todaro, 1989, 1994). By those strategies, the domestic firms (including foreign and indigenous firms) are protected from fierce competition from overseas firms. Consequently, imports of certain goods and services will have to be banned or their flow into a particular LDC has to be strongly limited. The rationale is that the protected domestic firms should have time, for e.g. to learn their business, to reap benefits of large scale production with lower unit costs and create strong backward and forward linkages (cf. Todaro, 1994).

However, there are critics who oppose any country's attempt to restrict trade. Most arguably, it is held that the cost of the protection of firms are higher than any expected benefits from such a measure. Instead, countries are advised to promote export-promotion (EP) strategies which reinforce free world trade and also bring much benefits to all countries (Todaro, 1989; Economist, 1994a: pp.3-46). For instance, a country with smaller domestic market will stand to gain from the larger world market. Debates about which approach is effective to boost the development of local industries, have, according to Todaro (1989), been going on for over 30 years. In practice, however, LDCs have adopted both IS and EP strategies with different degrees of emphasis at different times *(ibid.,* p.428).

It is argued in this paper that the role of the micro-economic units (e.g. manufacturing firms) in the successful implementation of whatever strategy (IS or EP) a country adopts to boost local industries' development needs be examined. An appropriate question to be addressed in this regard is as follows: how much do we know about the responsiveness of the specific actors which are expected to be the driving force behind the success of a country's infant industry promotion efforts?

The purpose of this article, therefore, is to deepen our understanding of the impact of the exchange relationships between MNCs and their indigenous suppliers in the process of promoting infant industries in LDCs. We delimit the setting of our investigation by focusing on Ghana. The country presents an interesting example of LDCs' vigorous attempt to promote infant industries.

Emphasis on Infant Industries in Ghana

As Todaro (1989: p.429) reports, Ghana embarked on the pursuit of her "Infant-Industry Protection" strategy already in the early 1960s. This led to the government's own active investment in establishing indigenous companies and, by a combination of measures (cf. Fieldhouse, 1978), to the attraction of MNCs to come into the country to produce commodities which had previously been imported into Ghana.

As a means to wean the country from its heavy dependence on imports of certain consumer and producer goods which may not only exacerbate its terms of trade with the outside world, but also inhibit the achievement of other objectives such as the need to create job opportunities, to generate internal sources of revenue needed for development, and to diversify into exportable manufactured goods/services active infant industry promotion has been pursued by successive governments, with diverse approaches over the years. The emphasis on the infant industry promotion stems from the great concern about the enormous consequences of so one-sided an economy. Three primary commodities, namely, cocoa, timber and minerals (e.g. gold, diamond, bauxite and mangenese) account for 70% of Ghana's foreign exchange earnings (cf. Ghana Exporters' Directory, 1991: p. 10).

The vigorous attempt by Ghana to attract foreign direct investment (FDI) and to also promote indigenous firms will have to be examined in terms of how specific demand for manufactured outputs or a concrete supply of specific production inputs is realized through time. This paper argues that certain specific actors, especially firms, controlling specific resources and performing specific activities are involved in the process of the expected linkage.

In Ghana certain MNCs were not only compelled by the government's commitment to import-substitution policies to switch on to local production, the MNCs were given certain incentives such as tariff protection, tax concessions in the earlier years, guarantees for the safety of foreign property and state action to provide essential services (Fieldhouse, 1978). An example of an MNC which enjoyed similar incentives as above, at least in the earlier years, in Ghana is the Unilever. In compliance with the Ghanaian government's import-substitution policy, Unilever had to, in 1963, establish its subsidiary, Lever Brothers Ghana, to produce soaps locally *(ibid.* pp. 416-417).

Once established, Lever Brothers Ghana (LBG) would need certain production inputs, some of which could be produced locally., Hence, as expected to be done to all MNCs in Ghana, certain local suppliers of production inputs for LBG had to be promoted. This was in line with the

pursuit of the import-substitution policy. LBG's suppliers which are of interest here are the Ghana Paper Conversion Corporation (GPCC), the Tema Food Complex Corporation (TFCC) and the Benso Oil Palm Plantation (BOPP). We shall return to these firms later on.

Effects of Regulations as well as Deregulation

Certain interventions, as Okoso-Amaa (1975) puts it, can be seen as timely actions, on the part of the government, to help or coerce certain interest groups in the society in such a way that more desirable results in business or in terms of the system's performance can be achieved. All the same, it has to be recognized that government interventions pose both constraints and opportunities for manufacturing firms, for example. There is an evidence of this timely intervention, on the part of the government, to promote local industries. The official ban of imports of hard soaps, in fulfillment of a promise, so that LBG could increase its projected volume of sales to 27,000 tons in 1964 and 32,500 tons in 1967 (cf. Fieldhouse, 1978: p.416) is an example of an active intervention to enhance the production of soaps by LBG. Restricting or prohibiting LBG, in turn, to import certain production inputs such as cartons, palm oil, palm kernel oil or tallow (a direct substitute oil to the last two products) was also meant to protect the indigenous suppliers of LBG.

While importers of soaps might have complained about the government's intervention in favour of LBG (see above), LBG too, came to regard its restrictions to import cartons or oils from markets which might have provided good quality products at competitive prices, for e.g. as an "anti-productive" measure against it. Taken together, we realize that government interventions may have varied and differential impacts on all economic agents in the society. Different governments intervene[†] in

[†] *Most of these interventions can be seen to be the government's constant attempt to establish its legitimacy in the eyes of some interest groups in the society (cf. Jansson and Sharma, 1993). The real socio-economic benefits from such interventions for all could be very remote.

the economic activities to the extent that sometimes far more harm than good is than to manufacturing firms, the driving forces behind the import-substitution idea.

In Ghana, one significant impact of the state's control of many activities results in the restriction of the freedom of action of most finns. For the most part in the 1960s and the 1970s, many firms did not have, inter alia, the freedom to import critical production inputs, have free access to foreign exchange and even have the right to price their own products. The effect was that the entire manufacturing sector's contribution, for e.g. to Ghana's GDP fell from 22% in 1973 to under 5% in 1983. The above fact and other problems such as a huge balance of payments deficit, high inflation rate of over 120% in the early 1980s, heavy external debts and lack of diversification in the economy forced a change of attitude among the country's policy makers (cf. Roe, 1991; Ghana Exporters' Directory, 1991). Since 1983, Ghana has embarked on comprehensive economic recovery and/or structural adjustment programmes (cf. Ghana: Handbook of Commerce and Industry, 1988).

The implementation of the above programmes has called for such measures as trade liberalization, reduced state expenditure, elimination of most controls and removal of subsidies in many areas. Such measures have had different effects on all economic agents in the country, particularly manufacturing firms (cf. Roe, 1991; World Development Report, 1990, 1994; Panford, 1994). For some manufacturing firms, so much has changed very fast during this short period of liberalization of trade that their ability to cope with new threats and/ or opportunities, which emerge from the increased competition, has weakened.

Although it is reported that the manufacturing sector, as a whole, has been increasing its contribution to the GDP, by 8% in 1986; by 10% in 1989 (cf. Roe, 1991: p.512), not all firms share this gradual recovery. Since the inception of the reforms, some of the domestic firms have disappeared from the market (cf. Daily Graphic, 1994: p.5; Tangari, 1992); others will soon follow, if they are not able to cope with events as they unfold.

The germane question now is how do we explain the forces which held LBG (the MNC) and its suppliers in focus here in the market during the time the Ghanaian economy was massively regulated? Similary, what is holding them in the present competitive and deregulated Ghanaian market? We seek the answers from the impact of the exchange relationships between them and other significant actors in their network.

Defining a Firm's Competence and how it Learns its Business

An MNC (here, LBG) and its indigenous suppliers (i.e. TFCC, GPCC and BOPP) must be able -- have the competence --to produce their respective products, which are specific outputs to be demanded in the market or concrete supply of production inputs, in conformity to the society's expected results from the infant industry promotion process. This task is often beyond the capabilities of individual firms and their resources. It presupposes mutual learning and mutual competence building by the parties.

The existing literature does not present a coherent definition of the concept of competence (cf. Bandura, 1986; Ulvund, 1985; Bjerkens *et al.,* 1990). With regards to business firms, e.g. a firm's competence is referred to its ability to act with effectiveness and efficiency when it comes to the call to satisfy the needs and wishes of its customers (cf. Kloftsen, 1992; Bjerkens *et al.,* 1990). In an attempt to meet a demand made on a firm, a firm's competence will reflect how the skills, knowledge and attitude, for instance, of its members are appropriate for this purpose. However, such a competence cannot be seen as an exclusive development which occurs only within a firm, rather it is seen to be often enhanced by the mutual learning and experiences the firm engages in through its interaction with other significant actors in a network context. This later definition of the concept of competence is adopted in this paper.

By his review of learning in the literature, Dodgson (1993: pp. 376-378) does not only examine how the concept of learning is viewed by different disciplines, he asserts that the management and innovation literature has much more clear view on learning. Thus, learning is seen as a purposive quest to retain and improve competitiveness, productivity, and innovativeness in uncertain technological and market circumstances. As uncertainties become higher, so does the need for learning. The way learning has been defined here and elsewhere (Sullivan and Nonaka, 1986: pp. 129-131; Argyris and Schon, 1978; Morgan, 1986) are all useful for our understanding of the various ways the concept of learning is viewed.

However, a firm's or an organization's unilateral detection and correction of errors or acquisition of information in order to improve its competitiveness or reduce uncertainty -- an act of learning for e.g -- may be inadequate. The interdependent relationships between most of our firms suggest that a firm and its interacting partners engage in mutual learning (cf. Ford *et al.,* 1986: p.37). The emphasis is that the interacting parties are mutually involved in measures meant to improve the uses of their interrelated resources or the performance of their interdependent activities, in the detection of errors or acquisition and processing of information in order to reduce uncertainties and complexities of their common concern.

Methodology

This article is based on case studies conducted with three indigenous supplier firms (TFCC, GPCC, and BOPP) as well as with their common buyer (LBG). These firms were finally chosen, from among 13 companies which were interviewed during the first phase, for an in-depth study because of a number of reasons. For example, they are manufacturing firms, they have significant impact on each other (a detailed illustration of this will be shown later), accessibility to them was less difficult, and they were prepared to participate in the research project. It has to be mentioned that the case research method was deemed very appropriate in that it helped, inter alia, to increase our knowledge of an under-researched area. The first interviews with the companies were held during the period of 4th October - 4th December 1991.

Complementary interviews with the same companies were conducted during the period of 26th January - 25th March 1994. The complementary interviews held with the respective firms became necessary because it facilitated our study of a process, the competence development of the firms over time and/or the firms' role in the infant industry promotion effort, to which successive governments of Ghana have been vigorously committed. The complementary interviews also helped to clarify issues which appeared incoherent, after a comprehensive report of the first interviews with the firms had been written and copies thereof sent to the respective respondents.

In each of the companies (both the supplying and the buying firms) interviews were held with managers who have had long personal experience with the counterpart (i.e. the trade partner). Our empirical delimitation, therefore, is a reflection of the accounts given by the various managers who were interviewed. Similarly, government officials who were interviewed, in connection with this study, gave their accounts of the exchange relationships between their respective ministries and the focal companies which they were very much aware of. Taken together, it is not unlikely that the various respondents interviewed may not be aware of other important exchange relationships which may equally affect the focal firms' behavior, performance, and the extent to which they are responding to the infant industry promotion effort initiated by the Ghanaian government. Nonetheless, the delimitation was very necessary to allow effective and comprehensive study of our theme in focus.

Theoretical Framework

In Unger's (Unger, 1988) view, theories such as the neo-classical theory, the conventional development theory and diffusion model have been criticized for their insufficient analysis of the dynamic processes involved in the adoption of the import-substitution industrialization strategies in most LDCs. Essentially, the theories are said to share one thing in common. Thus, they underestimate the problem of developing entrepreneurial skills in the course of the adjustment processes taking place in many LDCs.

Relating Unger's point of view to the present purpose of this paper, we realize that there is very scanty knowledge of how the specific actors (e.g. MNCs attracted into LDCs and certain established indigenous firms) who are expected to be the driving force behind the infant industry promotion effort are able to cope with constraints and/or opportunities which are set into motion in the course of the adjustment processes.

The above urges us to seek for theories which will facilitate our understanding of how the actors, through actions and interactions with significant others, are able to cope with both constraints and opportunities as they unfold. For the present purpose, the industrial network approach provides very useful insights.

The Industrial Network Approach

The industrial network approach[‡] (for details, see e.g. Johanson *et al.*, 1994; Håkansson, 1982, 1989; Hammarkvist *et al.*, 1982), on which the present article draws so much, suggests that specific actors, e.g. firms, organizations and individuals, possess specific resources and perform specific activities which create exchange relationships among them (Hägg and Johanson, 1982). In that sense, the activities of one actor are always, more or less, dependent on the outcome of those of certain others. Hence, e.g. the competitiveness of a company lies in its long-term exchange relationships with others in a network, and the changes in different companies' role and position in a network (Johanson and Mattsson, 1987).

As argued by Forsgren (1989: pp. 142-144), the investment behavior of a firm is dictated, to a large extent, by its long-lasting exchange relationships with certain suppliers, customers and competitors. Moreover, exchange relationships are connected (Cook and Emersson, 1978); thus, an actor's relationships with its focal partners, for e.g., are contingent, positively or negatively, upon exchange in other relations. However, actors tend to develop their specific positions relative to others in the network. The positions, according to Mattsson (1985), provide an actor with power over the activities in the industrial field. This power, in turn, is based on actors' direct control over their own activities and their indirect control over activities through the relationships with others (Pfeffer and Salancik, 1978).

To deepen our understanding of the impact of the exchange relationships between multinational companies and their indigenous suppliers in the

---

[‡] *This approach draws, to a certain extent, on other theories such as the social network theory and the resource dependence theory (cf. Håkansson, 1989; Håkansson and Johanson, 1993; Anderson *et al.*, 1994).

process of promoting infant industries in LDCs, a modified model of the industrial network approach has been developed -- a model of competence development through a network of exchange relationships. The model serves as the theoretical base for our analysis of the present phenomenon. The modified model has been developed inductively by eliciting insights from the interplay between the industrial network model and the various .empirical data (both primary and secondary) which have been collected. Besides, the modified model takes account of the unique conditions and processes underlying the actors' actions and/or interaction with each other in an LDC, Ghana.

A firm's competence to do what is expected of it by actors with whom it interacts is, therefore, the core of the modified model.

A Model of Competence Development Through a Network of Exchange Relationships

The model, as depicted in Fig. 1, suggests that a firm's competence development is influenced by those with whom it interacts. This implies that a firm's competence development is, in large, influenced by three basic factors and the relationship between them: (a) the transfer of elements of exchange, viz. product/service, information, financial and social exchange, between interacting parties, (b) the mutual learning undertaken by the parties, and (c) the mutual adaptations the parties make. The interplay between the above factors is seen as a relational process which evolves over time.

Where the product/service of an actor becomes an input for another actor, for instance, the activation and integration of their interdependent resources or activities cannot be done without engaging in effective financial, information and social exchange (i.e. the elements of exchange). The relationship between the elements of exchange results in a number of benefits for the interacting parties. Through the regular and effective transfer of such elements of exchange to and from a counterpart, for e.g., an actor's knowledge about the characteristics and expectations of its counterpart(s) will be enhanced. Moreover, the interacting parties will learn about how to utilize each other's capabilities and how to individually or mutually respond quickly to threats or opportunities which may have effects on their exchange relationships.

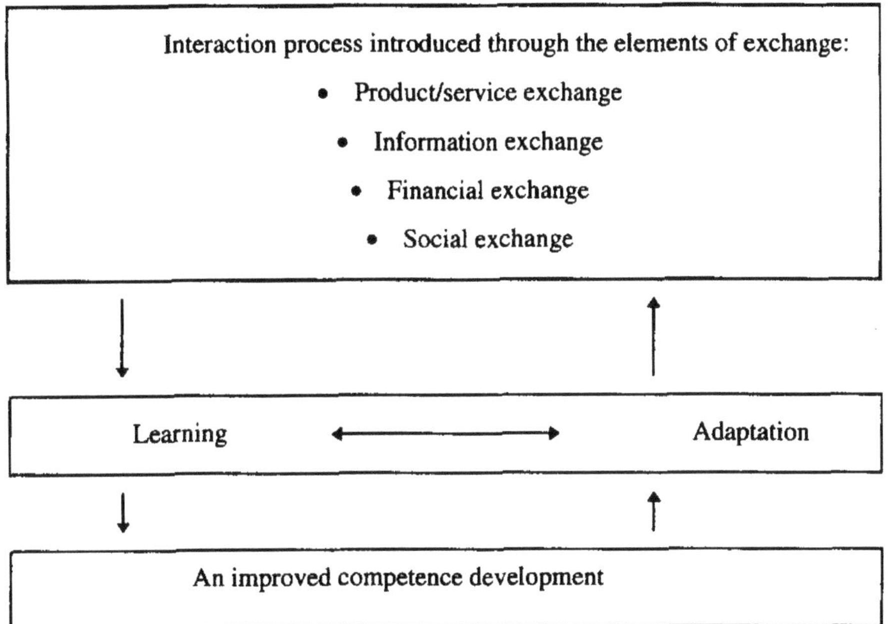

Figure 1. Competence Development Through a Network of Exchange Relationships

The social relationship, for e.g., does not only help to increase the interacting actors' knowledge of each other, it also contributes greatly to the co-operation, understanding and trust which strengthen the various bonds (cf. Hammarkvist *et al.,* 1982; Hägg and Johanson, 1982) between the firms for which they work.

The process of interaction denotes learning (Ford *et al.,* 1986). Principally, interacting parties strive after knowledge which helps them to take advantage of opportunities or overcome constraints which might inhibit their mutual exchange. Hence, a firm's unilateral detection and correction of errors, by the performance of certain activities, and/or acquisition of heterogeneous information in order to reduce uncertainties may not be adequate. As the results of the interdependent relationships between most firms, interacting parties do engage in mutual learning; for the ability to meet demands of others are often beyond the skills and/or resources of a single finn. The characteristics of interacting actors, their expectations, the combination and uses of heterogeneous resources, actions of the actors and so on may not be constant over time. They change, and so do the knowledge of the actors.

Changes in the network, in whatever form they occur, may call for certain mutual adaptations from the parties. Adaptation, in turn, influences the actors' learning rate. One adapts to a counterpart or a situation which demands mutual action from interacting parties, monitors the progress of the change and records the outcome of it -- be it negative or positive -- for future references in decision making. When an actor adapts to match the needs or capabilities of other actors, the former and the latter may become increasingly dependent on each other (cf. Hägg and Johanson, 1982; Håkansson and Snehota, 1995). All this is evidence that exchange relationships between certain actors have a history (cf. Snehota, 1990).

Finally, a firm's ability to meet demands made on it -- its competence -- stems from the interplay between the basic factors discussed above. As a firm's competence to meet its obligations increases through time, its exchange relationships, characterized by the transfer of elements of exchange, learning and adaptations, with other actors will be positively affected (see Fig. 1).

With the help of the above model, we shall illustrate and/or analyse the impact of the exchange relationships between an MNC and its indigenous suppliers in the process of promoting infant industries in Ghana.

The Processes of Promoting Infant Industries in Ghana: an Empirical Illustration

The processes through which the focal firms develop their respective competence in order to fulfill, for e.g, their role as import-substitution firms is highlighted by the analysis of the impact of the exchange relationships between MNCs and their indigenous suppliers in the process of promoting infant industries in LDCs. The impact of the complex and dynamic exchange relationships between Lever brothers Ghana (LBG), an MNC, and its indigenous suppliers, namely, The Tema Food Complex Corporation (TFCC), The Ghana Paper Conversion

Corporation (GPCC) and The Benso Oil Palm Plantation (BOPP) are examined.

TFCC: is an agro-industrial firm devoted to food and animal processing. TFCC was established and owned wholly by the government, as an import-substitution firm, in the early 1960s. It's focal product sold to LBG is palm kernel oil. TFCC sells 70% of its palm kernel oil to LBG. TFCC is not only one of the biggest firms processing food and animal feed in Ghana, it is also the leading producer of palm kernel oil in the country. LBG needs TFCC's palm kemel oil for its production of, e.g. detergent soaps and cooking oil. With the exception of flour, palm kernel oil accounts for much of TFCC's total profits after sales (i.e. Revenue - cost), when all its products, about 20, are considered.

GPCC: processes packaging materials. GPCC was established and owned wholly by the state, as an import-substitution firm in the early 1960s. GPCC had been the only producer of packaging materials in Ghana, until the recent entry of competitors in the 1990s in the producing and marketing of cartons. In the 1990s, GPCC is still one of the leading producers of cartons in the country. Carton is the focal product GPCC sells to LBG. LBG absorbs 50% of the entire cartons produced by GPCC. LBG needs cartons to package almost all its assorted products (see below).

BOPP: is an agro-industrial firm, producing mainly palm oil. BOPP is the third largest among the four leading producers of palm oil in Ghana, each of which sells about three quarters of its palm oil to the same buyer, LBG. 90% of BOPP's palm oil, the focal product, is sold to LBG. BOPP was established in the early 1980s as a purely private company. The Ghanaian government is even one of its shareholders. Palm oil is said to be the principal raw material for the production of LBG's detergents, especially hard soaps. A particular brand among the hard soaps, the so called key pale, accounts for 50% of LBG's annual total turnover. One will therefore understand why the marketing manager of LBG asserts that the oil is so basic to their production that, if they do not get good quality oils, they may ruin their business.

LBG: is a subsidiary of the Unilever Ghana Limited (UNIL). UNIL had to establish its subsidiary (i.e. LBG) in Ghana in the early 1960s because the then government in power actively promoted infant industries, thereby restricting imports of many goods such as UNIL's soaps into Ghana. It has already been pointed out that LBG and its suppliers in focus have, at different times, as import-substitution firms, enjoyed government protection of various kinds. Today LBG is regarded as one of the largest companies, in terms of either capital investment or employment, in Ghana (cf. Roe, 1991: p. 526). Presently, LBG does not only produce soaps, it has diversified products which fall under three main product areas: (1) detergents and/or non-soapy detergents, (2) edible fat oils, and (3) personal care products. It has also been shown that each of the indigenous suppliers in focus (see above) supplies a considerable amount of their respective focal products to LBG. All this confirms the importance of the exchange relationships between LBG (the MNC) and the indigenous suppliers.

What the MNC and its suppliers here have learned about their respective businesses, and the processes underlying the kind of competence each has been able to develop over the years so as to meet the primary objective of the Ghanaian government's vigorous promotion of infant industries is the next thing to highlight.

An Analysis of a Firm's Competence Development: the Impact of the Elements of Exchange, Learning and Adaptation Processes on the LBG-Suppliers Exchange Relationships

In the course of time, especially in the latter part of the 1970s and the early 1980s, LBG had to face one of the major challenges of its time. It was officially prohibited to import cartons, palm oil, palm kernel oil and/or tallow -- a direct substitute product to the last two oils. An obvious consequence, for e.g., was that LBG's wider international supplier-network of relationships was summarily reduced to only the smaller LBG-- Suppliers Network in Ghana.

Hence, LBG's ability to maintain its strong position, especially in the soap market, over time has become a function of LBG's competence to source the critical inputs in focus, its effective development of exchange relationships with the local suppliers and/or the local suppliers' ability to provide the critical inputs. The processes through which the actors, in different situations and time, complement each other in the pursuit of their respective goals is the thrust of this section. LBG has had stable and regular exchange relationships with TFCC since 1980. GPCC and LBG have had exchange relationships with each other since 1965. LBG's established exchange relationship with BOPP dates back to 1982.

LBG and each of its suppliers benefit much from the stable, long-lasting exchange relationships between them. The knowledge and/or experience which the parties have accumulated in dealing with each other facilitate the transfer of elements of exchange (i.e. product/service, information, financial and social exchange), the long-term mutual learning the parties engage in and mutual adaptations they make. All this enhances one actor's ability -- competence -- to meet demands made on it by others over time.

LBG and each of its suppliers lay strong emphasis on regular and close contacts with each other. Nearness to each other, especially visits to the partner's factory, and the regular contacts enable the parties to learn much more about what the counterpart may be doing, its capabilities, as well as constraints which can hamper the counterpart's fulfillment of a demand made on it. Thus, the parties do not deal with each other instrumentally, where the buyer, for e.g., sends an order with whatever specifications and hopes that the counterpart should be able to deliver the goods/services. For each of the suppliers, meeting the requirement of LBG, often expressed in the quality, competitive price, reliable and frequent delivery of a particular product, calls for regular and close contacts.

As the result of the frequent and/or rapid changes in LBG's product specifications -- mostly due to its attempts to withstand competition by offering good quality products at competitive prices in the market, producing palm oil or cartons for LBG becomes very complex. The parties often need to come together to discuss issues such as the cost involved in producing a given quantity of a particular product and how to ensure that the product being demanded fits the buyer's specifications. Since the characteristics of LBG's input products and market conditions, for e.g., keep changing all the time, both the buyer and the seller have the mutual task to ensure that they both benefit from the outcome of the exchange. This has been the major principle underlying LBG's close and regular relationships with its suppliers. This affects, inter alia, the way the parties learn from and/or adapt to each other.

There are examples of each of the suppliers' steady improvements in product quality and efforts to reduce cost of production, measures deemed necessary to match the ever changing needs of LBG. TFCC, for e.g., has installed a modern palm kernel oil refining machinery which allows TFCC to meet the high quality requirement of LBG and also to produce at least cost. BOPP is constantly upgrading the quality of its palm oil in order to meet the unstable quality needs of LBG. GPCC does not only strive to use up-to-date quality paper in the production of cartons, it is doing all it can to produce cartons at a relatively cheaper cost. Since packaging materials are very important for LBG, the two firms (i.e. GPCC and LBG) do sometimes engage in joint development and production of new cartons -- quite innovative products. By such team works, experts at GPCC do not only work closely at the same factory with experts from LBG, but also even experts from Unilever's headquarters (i.e. LBG's parent company) do participate in such joint projects.

LBG's quality control experts are occasionally supplied with samples of the supplier's respective products. The idea is to allow the quality controllers, research and development personnel, production and sales personnel, for e.g., to closely work together as a team to monitor quality. Thus, whenever the quality controllers examine samples of a particular product at LBG's laboratory, the same samples, say of palm kernel oil or palm oil, will be examined by the corresponding experts at the selling firm. Whatever results the experts come up to -- defect free samples or defected samples-- will have to be conveyed to all personnel who are, one way or the other, involved in the development, production, sale and purchase of the product in question'. This influences the parties way of learning from each other and/or adapting to each other so as to jointly clear bottlenecks which may be beyond the solution of a counterpart.

For example, there are occasions when LBG adapts to the financial bottlenecks which may hamper GPCC's purchase of enough paper from overseas, payment for which is made in hard foreign currencies. The paper is the core input of GPCC's cartons, products needed badly by

LBG (the buyer). Since a shortage of paper may have serious consequences for both GPCC and LBG, the latter sometimes buys paper for the former to produce cartons for it for a fee. This has even made LBG establish exchange relationships with its suppliers' (i.e. GPCC) suppliers in Europe, a relationship through which LBG gets certain desirable services.

To encourage or to adjust to its suppliers' product quality improvements which may benefit both the buyer and the seller, LBG gives each of them a premium whenever a good quality product is delivered. This is essential, for cost of improvement can sometimes be very high. However, a bad product attracts no premium. LBG may even reject a very bad product. This can be seen as a way of pressurizing or coercing a supplier to deliver good quality products.

Owing to various reasons such as the low purchasing power of the masses, the general low liquidity in the economy and "aggressive" competition in the market, both active and potential consumers of LBG' s products will have to be maintained and/or won by offering good quality products at affordable prices. More often than not LBG's sale of its products can be very slow, due to reasons such as above. Each of the suppliers adjusts to LBG by granting the latter the longest credit period as well as the maximum sum of credit as means to help LBG get enough time to sell its products and obtain money. Even if LBG is unable to pay for goods purchased at the expiry of the given credit period, a supplier can wait, until things get better for LBG.

The exchange relationships between LBG and its suppliers are, however, not devoid of the exercise of power by one actor over the counterpart. Inspired by different circumstances, to which the parties are exposed at different times and the pursuit of both common and conflicting interests, an exercise of power sometimes becomes inevitable. As expressed by some of the suppliers, LBG at times tries to utilize its position as a dominant buyer to dictate the terms of trade, particularly price, in its favour. This fact makes it extremely necessary for some of the suppliers in focus to co-operate with their direct competitors in negotiating prices and other terms of trade with LBG. Such a collective action does not only enable the parties to reach a consensus on fixing prices, for e.g., at a particular time, but it also becomes a counterforce which can neutralize LBG's dominant position vis-á-vis a single supplier.

Last but not the least, are the extensive and regular contacts between the firms in focus and other actors such as the government, certain relevant ministries, trade representatives (e.g. the Association of Ghana Industries, and the Ghana Chamber of Commerce) and other manufacturing firms. As stated elsewhere, government regulation or deregulation policies do bring with them constraints as well as opportunities. Where certain constraints emerge for a particular firm or firms, as the result of a government policy, the firm(s) may find it extremely difficult to get the government to alter its policy in favour of the complaining firm(s) without a collective action from several other actors.

For example, LBG and some of its suppliers in focus have been very active in taking the initiatives, at certain times to get their common trade representatives, other manufacturing firms and relevant ministries to address constraints which firms may face by the implementation of certain government policies, examples being adverse effects of import controls as well as of the "over-liberalization" of trade. Without the collective voice of such actors, a single firm may spend much time and energy to frequent the offices of government agencies, it may not get the attention of the government.

Discussions

The purpose of this article has been to deepen our understanding of the impact of the exchange relationships between MNCs and their indigenous suppliers in the process of promoting infant industries in LDCs. An important rationale behind the infant industry promotion argument is that domestic firms (including both MNCs and indigenous ones), whose role it is to help fill the cells in the input and output table of an LDC because these are virtually empty (cf. Caves, 1982), need be protected (see Introduction). The empirical evidence of how such high expectations of the society comes into fulfilment through the role played by certain specific actors, controlling specific resources and performing specific activities is lacking. The present paper therefore increases our knowledge in that regard.

Judging by the exchange relationships between LBG and its suppliers in focus, Ghana's massive efforts to promote infant industries have been successful. As the result of the indigenous companies' increased competence, through time, LBG's need to import any of the respective products of its suppliers is no more tenable, a strong purchasing position taken by LBG today. Since LBG too does not need to create and maintain, for instance, enormous storage facilities for imported palm oil, palm kernel oil or cartons -- not to mention the hazards and/or costs of importation and of storage in general – it has also improved markedly in its competence in procuring critical production inputs. This is very important because most firms are found to spend a substantial amount of their total cost on purchasing (cf. Gadde and Håkansson, 1993).

In the initial stages, LBG had problems with the kind of services it received from the indigenous suppliers in focus. Thus, assessing by the quality, the volume of supplies, prompt and reliable deliveries, and the competitive prices of the products, none of the suppliers' offer measured up to LBG's standards. The problem was compounded by the fact that LBG could not always obtain the Ghanaian government's permission to import any of the goods in question. However, investing enough resources in the establishment, maintenance and development of continuous, stable exchange relationships with its suppliers in question, LBG contends now that the investment has been yielding positive results. The quantity of each of the suppliers' products, especially palm oil and palm kernel oil, exceeds LBG's demand. The respective quality and price of the suppliers' products are now comparable to international standards. All this has made LBG change its purchasing strategy; the emphasis is now on local sourcing.

The effects of such a save in the imports of palm oil, palm kernel oil and cartons on the Ghanaian economy is considerable. It has, inter alia, employment, linkage, income and tax-effects. By not importing these products, Ghana also gains in saving foreign exchange and improving upon its balance of payments. LBG, for e.g., is currently exporting soaps made in Ghana to Cuba, while exporting glycerin, a by-product of soaps, to Europe. On top of that, LBG has 180 active distributors of its diversified products in Ghana; these distributors, in turn, do have linkages with several other actors along the distribution channel. Each of the suppliers in focus too has not only other customers, but has also linkages to certain suppliers in Ghana.

Can we generalize the success of Ghana's infant industry promotion efforts from this discussion? The answer is no. The performance of other domestic firms (i.e. both MNC and indigenous) in several other industries or branches need be equally examined so as to ascertain the extent to which they fulfil the import-substitution aspirations of the society. Our contention is that government interventions such as the restricting or the banning of imports of certain goods and services in order to protect domestic firms may or may not always be positive.

The protection of firms can be negative in that some firms may have no incentive to innovate, to improve upon product quality, to invest in efficient and least cost of production methods which may reduce the prices of their final products and to even produce adequately to meet the ever increasing and heterogeneous needs of society. Should that happen, then, the cost of protection becomes very high. Where the protection of local firms poses serious constraints on both the external and internal trade of the state, the cogent solution becomes the tearing down of all barriers or prohibitions which have outlived their usefulness. In this regard, the domestic firms' competence to cope with eventual competition cannot be decoupled from their historical and continuous exchange relationships with certain significant actors such as trade partners.

In Ghana, the process of dismantling trade barriers and the removal of most controls, since 1983, have all had profound adverse effects on firms which are not well equipped to face the emerged competition and other challenges. Several of the state-owned firms which were established about the same time as GPCC and TFCC and also many privately-owned firms have been closed down because of the tough competitive pressures they faced (cf. Panford, 1994; West Africa, 1994: p.1350).

Conclusion

This paper has shown that the pursuit of infant industry development, which in most LDCs are realized through import-substitution policy measures, involves specific actors who control specific resources and/or perform specific activities. However, the actors (e.g. the firms, the government and so on) who are drawn into the processes of promoting infant industries do not perform their respective activities in isolation; they are embedded in a network of exchange relationships.

The network thought explored in this article has provided us with very useful insights on how actors utilize the capabilities of each other. To this end, we say that the achievement of LBG and its suppliers in focus is attributable, on the one hand, to their intensive, regular and stable mutual exchange relationships with each other and, on the other, to their interaction with other significant actors in their wider network.

References

Anderson, J. C. (1994) Dyadic business relationships within a business network context. *Journal of Marketing* 58, 1-15.

Argyris, C. and Schon, D. (1978) *Organizational Learning: A Theory of Action Perspective.* Addison -Wesley, MA.

Bandura, A. (1986) *Social Foundations of Thought and Action: A Social Cognitive Theory.* Prentice-Hall, Inc., Englewood Cliffs, New Jersey.

Bjerkens, G., Dahlbom, B. and Mathiassen (eds) (1990) *Organizational Competence in System Development." A Scandinavian Contribution.* Student Literature, Lund.

Caves, R. E. (1982) *Multinational Enterprise and Economic Analysis.* Cambridge University Press, Cambridge.

Cook, S. K. and Emersson, R. M. (1978) Power, equity, commitment in exchange networks. *American Sociological Review* 43(October), 721-738.

Daily Graphic (1994) 2 February, 5, Accra.

Dodgson, M. (1993) *Organizational Learning: A review of some literatures,* Organization Studies, 14/3, Walter de Gruyter, Berlin/New York.

Economist (1994a) Global Economy Survey. 1-7 October, 3-46.

Economist (1994b) 12 November, 22.

Fieldhouse, D. K. (1978) *Unilever Overseas. The Anatomy of a Multinational, 1895-1965.* Croom Helm, London.

Ford, D. I. (1986) How do companies interact?. *Industrial Marketing and Purchasing* 1(1), 26-41.

Forsgren, M. (1989) Foreign acquisitions: internalization or network interdependency? In *Advances in International Marketing,*

Vol. 3, pp, 141-159. JAI Press Inc., Greenwich, Connecticut and London.

Gadde, L. E. and Håkansson, H. (1993) *Professional Purchasing.* Routledge, New York.

Ghana Exporters' Directory (1991) *World Wide Press Ltd.* Accra.

Ghana: Handbook of Commerce and Industry (1988/89) *Ministry of Trade and Tourism.* Accra.

Hammarkvist, K.-O. *et al.* (1982) *Marknadsf6ring for Konkurrenskrafts* (Marketing for Competitiveness). Liber, Stockholm.

Håkansson, H. (1982) *International Marketing and Purchasing of Industrial Goods: An Interaction Approach.* John Wiley and Sons, Chichester.

Håkansson, H. (1989) *Corporate Technological Behaviour. Co-operation and Networks.* Routledge, London.

Håkansson, H. and Johanson, J. (1993) The Network as a Governance Structure, Interfirm Cooperation Beyond markets and Hirarchies. In *The Embedded Firm, The Socio-Economics of Industrial Networks,* ed. G Grabher, pp. 35-55. Routledge, London.

Håkansson, H. and Snehota, I. (1995) *Developing Relationships in Business Networks.* Routledge, London.

Hägg, I. and Johanson, J. (eds.) (1982) *Fgretag i Niitverk* (Firms in Network). SNS, Stockholm.

Jansson, H. and Sharma, D. D. (1993) Industrial Policy liberalization and TNCs: the Indian experience. *Scandinavian Journal of Management* 9(2), 129-143.

Johanson, J. and Associates (1994) Internationalization, Relationships and Networks, Acta Universitatis Upsaliensis. Studia Oecenomiae Negotiorum, 36, Uppsala University, Sweden.

Johanson, J. and Mattsson, L.-D. (1987) International relations in industrial systems: a network approach compared with the transaction cost approach. *International Studies of Management and Organization,* XVII(i), 34-48.

Killick, T. (1981) *Policy Economics: A Textbook of Applied Economics on Developing Countries.* Heinemann, London.

Kloftsen, M. (1992) Tidiga utvecklingprocesser i tekniskbaserade frretag. Dissertation, Department of Management and Economics, Linktiping, Sweden.

Mattsson, L.-G. (1985) An application of a network approach to marketing -- defending and changing market positions. In

Dholakai, N., and Arndt, J., (eds.). *Changing the Course of Marketing: Alternative Paradigms for widening Marketing Theory. Research in Marketing Supplement 2,* eds N. Dholakai and J. Arndt. JAI Press, Greenwich, CT.

Morgan, G. (1986) *Images of Organization.* Sage Publications, Inc., Great Britain.

Okoso-Amaa, K. (1975) *Rice Marketing in Ghana: An analysis of government intervention in business.* Scandinavian Institute of African Studies, Uppsala.

Panford, K. (1994) Structural adjustment, the state and workers in Ghana: an African development. *A Quartely Journal of the Council for the Development of Social Science research.* Codesria, Dakar.

Pfeffer, J. and Salancik, G. R. (1978) *The External Control of Organizations: A Resource Dependence Perspective.* Harper Grow, New York.

Roe, A. R. (1991) Economy. In *Regional Survey ofthe World: Africa South of Sahara (1992),* 21st Edition. Europa Publications Ltd, London.

Snehota, I. (1990) Notes on a theory of business enterprise. Dissertation, Department of Business Studies, University of Uppsala, Sweden.

Sullivan, J. J. and Nonaka, I. (1986) The application of organizational learning theory to Japanese and American management. *Journal of International Business Studies,* Fall, 127-147.

Srdersten, B. (1970) *International Economics.* Macmillan Press Ltd, London/New York.

Tangari, R. (1992) The Politics of government -- business relations in Ghana. *The Journal of Modern African Studies* 30, 97-111.

Timmermann, V. (1982) *Entwicklungstheorie und Entwicklungspolitik.* Vandenhoeck and Ruprecht, Grttingen.

Todaro, M. P. (1989) *Economic Development in the Third World,* 4th Edn. Longman Publishing, New York.

Todaro, M. P. (1994) *Economic Development,* 5th Edn. Longman Publishing, New York.

Ulvund, S. E. (1985) Cognitive development in infancy: a collection of theoretical and empirical studies. Dissertation, Oslo.

Unger, K. (1988) Industrial structure, technical change and micro-economic behaviour in LDCs. In *Technical Change and*

Economic Theory, eds Dosi *et al.* Pinter Publishers, London/New York.

West Africa (1994) 1-7 August, p.1350.

World Development Report (1994) *Infrastructure for Development.* Published for the World Bank, Oxford University Press, Oxford/New York/Toronto.

World Development Report (1990) *Poverty, Published for the World Bank.* Oxford University Press, Oxford/New York/Toronto.

Received July 1995
Revised March and July 1996

Chapter Four

The Search For Foreign Direct Investment (FDI): The Case Of Ghana. A Paper Presented At EISAM's Workshop On International Strategy & Cross Cultural Management In Vienna, September 29-30, 2005.

Abstract

That foreign direct investment (FDI) is a valuable undertaking that all nations strive to attract and sustain is well known and well discussed in the literature. However, a systematic study and/or analysis of how some countries invest much in attracting FDI, but with poor results, is lacking. This paper contributes by analyzing the incessant efforts which countries make to attract FDI but with very dissatisfying results. One important conclusion from this study is that while a country uses numerous incentives and alleged macro and micro policies as means to bring in much FDI, potential investors might not respond because they might be thinking about areas where they could profitably and securely put their resources to use. Ghana is a case in point when looking at a country that has not succeeded well, in spite of its investments in attracting FDI.

Keywords: FDI, FDI attraction, incentives, macro and micro policies, Ghana

Introduction

Owing to the scarcity of resources of various types and the uncertainty about positive return on investment (Daniels & Radebaugh, 2001;

Hollensen, 2001) from foreign investment, a potential area to be chosen for direct investment would be a game of selectivity for potential investors. Hence, only a limited number of firms can afford to take to foreign investment. This suggests that only a few areas with high potentialities would be able to attract the limited number of foreign direct investors to a significant magnitude.

A recent report (Dagens Industri, Wednesday May 5, 2004: 15) shows that China's attractiveness as the world's production centre and India's attractiveness as the centre for administrative and financial services respectively are drawing massive investors into these areas. Of the total FDI that went into developing countries last year, 60 % went to Asia, of which half of that went to China alone (p.15). The bulk of the FDI that flowed into the Third World between 1988 and 1992 landed in the 15 relatively rich countries. In Asia, China, topping all the 15 countries, received an average over $5 billion each year. Singapore with an annual inflow of $4.3 billion attracted the next largest FDI in Asia. Other beneficiaries in Asia that received much FDI during the period are, ranging from largest inflows to least, Malaysia, Thailand, Hong Kong, Taiwan, Indonesia, South Korea. In Latin America, Mexico, receiving $3.7 billion annually in FDI, was the third largest recipient among the 15 countries (The Economist, September 10-16, 1994:124).

The competition for FDI has always been very fierce (United Nations Report, 1978, p.237; Economist, June 20, 2001: 2; Economist, September 10-16, 1994:124; Ghana Drum, November, 1993: 31; Williams and Wint, 2002, p.363). This purports that the trend regarding the inflow of FDI to a few countries, as also revealed above, will continue, unless other nations that are competing for FDI also offer 'packages of value' that may draw potential investors to them.

In view of the above, the search and the inflow of FDI into certain countries have to be systematically analyzed. Hence, the germane questions that are addressed here are as follows: (1) Why and how does a country seek to attract FDI? (2) Wherein lies a country's comparative advantage (thus, its attractiveness) to win and sustain much FDI? and (3) Why have some countries not been successful in attracting much FDI as expected?

The purpose of this study is to deepen our understanding of how and why certain countries invest a lot of resources to attract FDI but have not had satisfactory results. However, our study and/or analysis are delimited to Ghana, a Less Developed Country, which has over the years invested much efforts and resources in attracting FDI.

Methodology

Insights have been drawn from a number of existing literatures, which discuss the phenomenon FDI in general, and the attraction of FDI into Ghana in particular. By drawing on the secondary sources, we will endeavor to illuminate Ghana's incessant efforts to win and sustain FDI and the results thereof. We will analyze Ghana's efforts by using the insights gained from the various perspectives on FDI inflow into certain countries. This will enable us to know the extent to which Ghana has been able to attract FDI and whether or not the country is satisfied with the FDI inflow, judged from the efforts being made towards that end. Hence, this study is basically based on secondary sources.

A brief review of the FDI literature

FDI is an area that has been extensively researched (Dunning, 1981; Teece, 1985; Hennart, 1982; Caves, 1982). A number of motives have been put forward to explain why investors undertake FDI (Dunning, 1981; Caves, 1982; Eriksson, 1990; Economist June 20, 2001). Investors will undertake FDI as a means to overcome some trade barriers such as transportation costs, high tariffs, restrictions on and/or ban on imports of certain goods and services by a government policy. FDI can also be undertaken as a means to lessen competition by buying it, displacing it or preempting competitors (Hennart, 1982; Armstrong, G, et al, 2002; Teece, 1985). Investors also use FDI as a means to exploit firm-specific advantages such as know-how, special skills and entrepreneurship (Griffin, R, et al, 1998; Dunning, 1981). Previous studies on FDI have produced a number of theories that aid our understanding of why and how investors would undertake FDI. Some of these theories warrant discussion here.

The internalization theory explaining FDI

This theory suggests that a firm may operate in an imperfect world where it is difficult to conduct certain transactions within the market. More especially when setting prices on certain intangible assets such as know-how, special skills and entrepreneurship is not possible because of the different perception of price-value combinations held by the buyer and the owner of the intangible asset; the owner would prefer to exploit those assets by itself. Hence, the owner would undertake FDI in order to take advantage of its firm-specific assets. Understanding this world view of the behaviour of potential FDI investors is very crucial in any effort to win them. However, the critics of such a model assert that, among other things, there is much emphasis on only the motives and the decision processes within the firm (how to gainfully exploit its firm-specific assets (Hollensen, 2001; Williams and Wint, 2002) that are difficult to trade in the marketplace. No or less attention is paid to the potential of host government policies and other factors, which can affect the benefits and costs of undertaking foreign (FDI). This has led to alternative theories that help us understand factors that might underlie why and how firms might choose to undertake FDI in a certain host country. The eclectic theory of international production is one of such theories.

The eclectic theory of international production

To understand why and where potential investors will undertake foreign direct investments (FDI), the eclectic theories of FDI have proved to be very useful, albeit there are some criticisms (Williams and Wint, 2002; Asante, et al, 2000; Hollensen, 2001). Dunning's (1981; 1993) eclectic theory of production is an example of such eclectic theories, very much cited in the literature of FDI. As argued in the theory, an investor's decision to engage in FDI in a particular host country will, in large, depend on the extent to which (1) it can gainfully exploit its firm-specific assets through the process of internalization, (2) the location attractions of the firm's country's endowments compared with those offered by other countries, and (3) governments' role in influencing international business patterns. The eclectic theory of production meets criticisms too. Among other things, emphasis is seemingly placed on the relative bargaining power of firms and national governments, thus ownership advantages versus location advantages, which influence why and where FDI will be made (see Williams and Wint, 2002). Another criticism is that the approach is predominantly concerned with manufacturing activities. The role of markets in motivating international expansion of a firm's activities are virtually not stressed (Johanson, et al, 1994).

As Alderson (1957) argued, what is common to all social science researchers is the desire to understand and to explain the totality of human behaviour, each contributing from the standpoint of his/her unique interest. Other researchers also underline the impossibility to have theories that can represent reality a 100 percent. "It must be reiterated that, as of now, it is difficult to find a clear theoretical framework which can stand on its own as the theory of foreign direct investment. However, the industrial organization approach seems to be the most pervasive in the literature. As Agarwal (1980:763) maintains, Dunning's 'eclectic' approach (1977, 1979), which considers FDI as dependent on ownership, internalization and locational advantages, provides some ray of hope for an integrated theory of FDI" (Asante, et al, 2000, p.12).

For this present study, Dunning's (1981; 1993) eclectic theory of production serves as the theoretical foundation on which the systematic analysis of why a country needs to attract FDI, how it attracts and sustains them, and on which the overall performance in winning and sustaining FDI is based. Some of the model's weaknesses, especially where market's role receives little or no attention, would be addressed.

A brief review of earlier studies on attracting FDI to developing countries

Asiedu's (2001) attempt to find out whether or not factors that affect FDI in developing countries affect countries in Sub-Saharan Africa (SSA) differently is very insightful. In her survey study using aggregate data from 71 developing countries, 32 from SSA and 39 non-SSA countries, Asiedu (p.108) aims to not only have a much larger sample, but to also include many African countries; previous studies had small samples. Asiedu tested the extent to which the determinants of FDI identified in previous studies explain the variation in FDI for her comprehensive sample. All in all, the work can be seen as a replication of previous studies; the author's larger sample used and the conclusions drawn from the study seem to differ, however, from previous studies.

Asiedu's (2001, pp.114-115) study offers four important results. Result number one states that, on the average, SSA countries received less FDI than countries in other regions by virtue of their geographical location; there is a negative effect on FDI for being an African country. Result two is that higher return on capital promotes FDI to SSA countries, but has no significant impact on FDI flows to SSA countries, ceteris paribus. Result number three shows that openness to trade is found to promote FDI to both SSA and non-SSA countries. However, it is asserted that the marginal benefit from increased openness is less for SSA – suggesting that trade liberalization will generate more FDI to non-SSA countries than SSA countries. For her, the lesser response of FDI to trade liberalization has to do with the fact that foreign investors do not perceive reform as credible; liberalization measures by governments are perceived as transitory and therefore subject to reversal. Finally, infrastructure development is said to promote FDI to non-SSA countries, but has no significant impact on FDI flows to SSA countries, ceteris paribus. "These results suggest that Africa is different" (p.116). Although the author presents a very insightful study, the aggregated statistical data makes it difficult to differentiate the African countries from one another in order to determine which country in the SSA countries have succeeded vis-á-vis others; knowing why and how some have succeeded but others have not would be interesting to note. Putting all countries in the same basket does not determine which country in SSA is satisfied with the FDI it is getting and which are not. This makes the assertion that Africa is different, in the attempt to attract FDI, quite debatable.

Williams and Wint's contribution: Attracting FDI to developing countries

In the review of existing literature on the topic at hand (Willimas and Wint, 2002), the authors report that previous studies indicated that promotion had a statistically significant impact on investment flows to the full sample of countries (18 developed and 32 developing countries), and to developed and developing countries tested separately in previous studies. Such a finding, as maintained, has been particularly encouraging to developing countries that are eager to attract FDI. This piece of information makes the assertion that Africa is different (see the Asiedu's study above) in the search and the ability to win FDI very debatable. However, over time, the promotional activities, as an important dimension of a country's differential advantage, has become a common practice among many competing countries in the attraction of FDI. This has prompted the authors to seek answers to the following questions:

> "Do promotional activities and liberal investment policies begin to lose their ability to differentiate one country over another, with respect to attracting FDI? Is there, in fact, a life cycle to the differential effectiveness of special programs that seek to attract investment?" (Williams and Wint, 2002, p.364)

> "Conceptually, if there are no policy differences among countries with respect to receptiveness to FDI, and the promotional programs of countries are equally effective (or equally ineffective), then no particular country will be able to use policies or programs to increase its share of incoming FDI flows" (Williams and Wint, 2002, p.365)

Williams and Wint (2002, pp.368-369) conducted a survey study, using their model of determinants of foreign direct investment flows, to find out the extent to which countries are able to differentially attract FDI through promotional activities. Some important findings are worth reporting here. Per-capita income has been a dominant factor explaining FDI flows; it dominates all other economic and non-economic variables (e.g. per capita income, interest rates, literacy rates, current account position and promotional activities) that were tested in the authors' (pp.366-370) study. Promotional activities, however, were found to be relatively insignificant. Since several countries converge toward best practice in promotion, the authors assert that it becomes difficult for any particular country to gain a differential advantage in relation to attracting FDI. However, the authors recommend that countries should not discontinue offering special promotional activities to attract FDI; they add up to efforts that lead to overall increase in FDI flows. Again, this is a very insightful study, yet the aggregate nature of the study limits its explanatory power (see also Williams and Wint, 2002, p.370).

Determinants of FDI in Ghana

Asante, et al, (2000), provide a country-specific study to discover factors that determine FDI into the country. Three different studies, econometric analysis, survey and interviews, were conducted in order to find out, using similar variables, what determines FDI flows into Ghana. A sample of 70 enterprises, 31 of domestic origin and 39 FDI-based firms were studied by the survey. Interviews were also conducted with 21 FDI-based firms (13 in manufacturing, 6 non-industrial and 3 in mining). Ten domestic firms in manufacturing were also interviewed. As admitted by the authors, to exactly measure the determinants of FDI have been extremely difficult due to problems of obtaining accurate data and respondents' reservations in giving some 'sensitive' information. Yet some important conclusions have been drawn by the authors. An important conclusion drawn, especially from the survey study, was that the incentive structure, availability of raw materials (in the case of mining and ore deposits), and market potential have had a dominant effect in the promotion of both domestic and direct foreign investment in Ghana (Asante et al, 2000, p.65). All in all, a final conclusion from all the three studies conducted is as follows:

> "Although, in the econometric approach, the market was found to exert either a negative or an infinitesimal positive influence on FDI, depending on the definition of the market, the survey results in contrast showed that the market factor ranked third after incentives and raw materials availability" (Asante et al, 2000, p.95)

> "The study also found from the survey and interviews that coherence and predictability in the implementation of policies are crucial for accelerating both domestic and foreign investment" (Asante et al, 2000, p.101)

Checking Asante et al's (2000) findings against Williams and Wint's (2002) findings, where promotional activities such as incentive structures were insignificant in the attraction of FDI to developing countries, the Asante et al's (2000) study provides an opposite picture, at least for Ghana. This is one of the reasons why aggregate studies, such as surveys, may conceal much information. The Asante et al's (2000, p.96) study reveals that incentives, an important component of the country's promotional activities, have played a crucial role in attracting FDI. From the three useful studies, all trying to increase our understanding of factors that determine FDI inflow into a host country, particularly a developing country, each study produces a different 'critical' or predominant factor, which is a driving force in bringing in FDI. There are many insights into the incessant efforts which countries have made over the years in order to attract FDI, but with dissatisfying results. This is the gap, which the present study, by using Ghana's example, seeks to fill. If many developing countries' economic policies and/or promotional activities are converging, as has been established in Williams and Wint's study (2002), we would expect countries to put more marketing thinking in their efforts to attract FDI. It is about offering 'packages of value' that stand out among the competing countries' offers. And as shown in the preceding sections, Ghana or countries in the developing world are not only competing among themselves, they are competing with all countries in attracting investors. Some recent trends illustrate where and why much FDI are flowing into certain areas more than the others.

Expected growth: In direct relation to the size of the market, investors are very much interested in growth opportunities. As stated elsewhere (Dagens Industri, Wednesday 5 May, 2004: 15), China has had an average growth of 8.1 percent for the last ten years and India has also shown the same trend in the year 2004. The effect of the growth has been that two million jobs within the financial services are expected to be flown from the Western World to India up to 2008. China has now become the fourth largest export country, after Germany, U.S.A. and Japan. However, half of the Chinese exports are produced by foreign firms (p.15). The example with India and China shows the relative importance of the expected growth of a host-country market.

Geography and natural resources: The geographic position of a host-country market can be very important in investors' decisions to undertake foreign investment there. Singapore, although a very small country, attracts many direct investments more than any other country in the Southeast Asian region (Economist, September 10-16, 1994:124). Singapore's nearness to other countries in the Southeast Asia region and to China and Japan is considered as a strategic and/or comparative advantage in its efforts to attract FDI. The availability of some important natural resources, such as oil and mineral resources, also explains why FDI that are meant to exploit such natural resources cost efficiently locate in certain host-country markets having useful natural resources (Asiedu, 2001; Asante et al, 2000; Daniels & Radebaugh, 2001).

Policy framework: Socio-economic and/or political policies of the host-country market can also be very decisive for investors when considering moving resources into the country. Governments can use fiscal and monetary policies (Armstrong, G., et al, 2002; Daniels & Radebaugh, 2001) in such a way that they intervene in the conduct of business that might put economic agents in a disadvantage when doing business in the host-country market. Malaysia is placed third after China and India, when looking at thousands of jobs that are created within the IT-Sector by foreign investors. Malaysia's attractiveness has to do with the country's access to qualified personnel, business climate and cost levels, well-developed infrastructure and a strong support from the government (Dagens Industri Wednesday 20 October, 2004: 17). All in all, a host-country's policy framework would be one of the important means to measure the level of risk in doing business in a particular host-country's market. One researcher has the following to say:

> "The underlying reality was that by the 1960s the profitability of any particular Unilever subsidiary in a less developed country was likely to be determined less by its efficiency or by the market than the government policy and the way this was implemented by the bureaucracy" (Fieldhouse, 1978, p. 601).

While potential investors are busy looking for where they can profitably invest their resources, the countries that need them also expect some benefits from FDI.

Benefits expected from FDI in a host country

Among other things, FDI will facilitate the production of goods and services that might lead to the generation of employment opportunities, bringing with it also managerial skills and technology (Asiedu, 2001, p.107). Governments' tax revenues are boosted as the result of the various linkage effects (Caves, 1982) that the generated production of goods and services bring with them. FDI also bring about competition in the market for input as well as output (Reuber, 1973). Hence, countries compete for FDI.

"A transfer of technology often accompanies FDI, as foreign firms introduce new technologies and management techniques to the host country. For example, the Japanese companies Mitsubishi and Toyota brought their lean manufacturing and JIT inventory systems to Australia when they built their manufacturing plants in Adelaide, South Australia and Altona, Victoria. Other Australian manufacturers, both in the motor vehicle industry and outside that industry, have adapted these techniques to their factories, boosting their productivity and profitability" (Griffin, R, et al, 1998, p. 132).

"So far as the governments of ASEAN states are concerned, the official stand is quite clear. Foreign investment, especially by MNCs, is not only welcome but much sought after. Every government in the region maintains expensive investment promotion offices in the major cities of industrial nations, and they post some of the best talents to these offices. Governments would not do such things if they had any reservations about the value of foreign investment and the important role MNCs could play in the development of their economies." (Swee, G.K., 1995, p.117)

However, the inflow of FDI into countries, as some of the preceding sections show, has favoured the richer developed countries and/or the relatively rich countries in the less developed countries (Williams and Wint, 2002; Economist, 1994:124). But FDI are not without problems when they establish in a host country (see below).

Some concerns about FDI

There is opposition to FDI (Daniels & Radebaugh, 2001; Griffin, R., et al, 1998). Among other things, there is the fear that the multinational companies that undertake FDI may out-compete their local competitors, the latter disappearing from the market as the result. It is also contended that the best resources may go to foreign companies. Some will even argue that expatriates may occupy the key managerial and technical positions. Such a situation may not contribute to the "learning-by-doing" process in host countries.

"FDI may result in foreign control of the national economy. Ownership of natural resources such as oil and natural gas, coal or mineral deposits by foreigners may mean that these non-renewable assets are exploited for the short-term gain of the foreigners, not in the long-term benefit of the host country's citizens." (Griffin, R., et al, 1998, p.133)

Evidently, the benefits and the costs for FDI can be long. Each country that seeks FDI will have to weigh the benefits against the costs of obtaining some FDI and maintaining them. Many researchers have indicated that the disadvantages and advantages of foreign investment in a country are difficult to measure accurately (Reuber, 1973; Eriksson, 1990). FDI can take many forms (Griffin, R., et al, 1998). Investors may choose to purchase existing assets in a host-country market. Investors can choose to undertake new investment in property, plant, and equipment. Investors can also participate in a joint venture with a local partner. In the next section we will discuss why and how Ghana, over the years, has invested in attracting FDI.

Ghana's efforts to attract FDI

Right from the beginning of the country's independence, successive governments have embarked on massive programmes and/or investments to attract FDI (Ghana: Handbook of Commerce and Industry, 1988/89; Business & Financial Times, November 13-November 30, 1991:8, Todaro, 1994; Asante et al, 2000). Ghana's need for FDI and its preparedness to offer incentives to foreign investors date back in the late 1950s, as the following quote illustrates.

> "The 1958 statement (which was similar to that of 1954) divided economic activities into three categories: (1) those reserved entirely to the Government, including railway transport, electricity generation for public sale, radio broadcasting, and the export of cocoa. (ii) those in which government participation was mandatory, including the manufacture of alcohol, narcotics, and alcoholic beverages; and (iii) those open to private

> enterprise, which covered 'the entire range of industries not included in the very limited schedule of those in the other 2 categories'. 'For industries in the third category', the Prime Minister said in a statement, 'I wish to emphasize that the government is determined to expand the industrial capacity of Ghana, and that private capital and technical know-how are welcome from any source, whether from within or from outside Ghana" (Garlick, 1971, p.119).

The search for the FDI could also be seen as a compulsion to some foreign firms that already had some trade with Ghana, long before the country attained its independence. The country's import-substitution policy that was in place during the late 1950s and the greater part of the 1960s (Todaro, 1994; Killick, 1981; Ghana: Handbook of Commerce and Industry, 1988/89) forced foreign firms such as Unilever to do FDI in Ghana.

> "It was perfectly happy with an export market that provided as much as £150,000 pre-tax profits in the 1950s and there is no indication in the records of hope that local production would provide a better return. But by the later 1950s the concern was faced with a stark choice: invest or probably lose an established import market to whatever enterprise, public or private, was allowed to set up the one large soap factory that Ghanaian market could support" (Fieldhouse, 1978, pp. 416-417).

Firms that did undertake FDI as the result of the government's implementation of the import-substitution policy did receive some protection from outside competition. The Prime Minister was said to have behaved as follows:

"Although he believed in state socialism, he also accepted that rapid development in the consumer goods sector depended on direct foreign investment, and he seemed willing to attract such investment by providing tariff protection, tax concessions in the earlier years, guarantees for the safety of foreign property and state action to provide essential services" (Fieldhouse, 1978, pp.412-413).

Fieldhouse (1978) also records that the Ghanaian government banned imports of hard soaps, in fulfillment of a promise, so that Lever Brothers Ghana (a subsidiary of Unilever) could increase its projected volume of sales to 27,000 tons in 1964 and 32,500 tons in 1967.

Certain local 'support industries', namely suppliers of raw materials, semi-finished products and finished products (Fieldhouse, 1978; Awuah, 1994) were promoted or established by the government to serve the needs of the foreign investors and a variety of industries that invested in local production. Unilever, for example, has been sourcing its need of palm oil, palm kernel oil, and cartons from industries that were purposely established to serve the needs of Unilever and the soap industry (Awuah, 1994).

The massive efforts to attract FDI in the 60s were met with little success (Asante et al., 2000, p. 29). In the 1960s until the early 1980s, the Ghanaian market was massively controlled with import control, price control, foreign exchange control, distribution control and so on (Ghana: Handbook of Industry and Commerce, 1988/89; Economic Digest, January 22-28, 1990: 3; Roe, 1991). On top of such control problems, economic agents faced problems such as high inflation rates at well over 120 %, high cost of borrowing from the banks, the devaluation of the cedi (the local currency), and limited markets (Business and Financial Times, January 27-February 9, 1994:4; West Africa, 1-7 August, 1994:1350; Ghana Exporters' Directory, 1991; Asante et al., 2000). Political factors also played a role to scare away investors; there was a massive intervention in the activities of private firms that destroyed the investment climate. The State was even accused of harassing businessmen (Panford, 1994, p. 80; Tangari, 1992, pp.100-101). All this contributed to erode the confidence that investors (Ghanaians and foreigners) had in Ghana as a place for investment (Asante et al, 2000).

In 1983, a new change of policy orientation brought into being the Economic Recovery Programme (ERP), followed by structural adjustment programmes, that Ghana had to undertake in order to come to terms with the problems enumerated above. One of the important measures to tackle the problems was and is to continue to win FDI into the country by the use of incentives. The ERP had the primary objective to eliminate large state deficit, abolish controls on price, interest rate, foreign exchange, and import. The local currency, cedi, had to be devalued and made flexible. Most state subsidies had to be removed completely and inflation rate reduced drastically. And above all, trade had to be liberalised (Roe, 1991; Newsweek, June 1992: 27; World Development Report, 1994, pp.48-49; Asante et al, 2000; Kuada and Sorensen, 2001). The growth that seemed to have come, as the reforms were undertaken, was seen by some critics as "aid-driven" (Ghana Drum, November, 1993:30; Dagens Nyheter, November 9, 1992). According to the critics, the implementation of the ERP and the huge inflow of foreign aid did not put Ghana in a better position. To successfully carry through the reforms suggested by the IMF/World Bank, in the long run, there was the cry for more FDI.

Ghana's bilateral investment protection agreement with Britain in March 1989 and the country's decision to join the World Bank's Multilateral Investment Guarantee Agreement (MIGA) are considered as a massive campaign, on the part of Ghana, to attract foreign direct investment (Financial Times, July 11, 1989:3; Asante et al, 2000). In the 21st century too, Ghana continues, through a number of incentives and guarantees plus investment opportunity areas, to attract foreign investors (Ghana Investment Promotion Centre, 2004). For example, under investment guarantees, there is the free transferability of capital, profits and dividends. It is even stated that all areas, especially the following: cotton and textiles, agro-processing, ethnic beauty products, floriculture, transport services, seafood processing, property development, tourism, ceramics, information technology/electronics, apparel, and hand tools, (page 2 of 2) are open to foreign participation.

The extent of investors' response to Ghana's search for FDI

Ghana, like many other countries in Africa, has not been able to attract much FDI. The following statistics show the situation Ghana faces. As reported elsewhere, the massive efforts to attract FDI (Asante et al, 2000) throughout the 60s proved less successful. Other facts, as reviewed below, also show how Ghana has performed poorly in attracting FDI over the years.

Net FDI (Millions of Dollars)

1980	1981	1982	1983	1984	1985	1986	1987	1988	1989	1990
16	16	16	12	2	6	4	5	5	15	15

Source: Ghana Drum, November, 1993: 31.

Comparing the above inflow of FDI into Ghana with those that went to Latin America between 1988 and 1992, for example, Ghana was not very successful. Between 1988 and 1992, FDI inflow into the following Latin American countries (The Economist, September 10-16, 1994:124) was: Mexico $ 3.7 billion, Argentina $2.1 billion, Brazil $1.5 billion and Venezuela $700 million and Columbia $500 million. Ghana's investment to attract FDI in recent times has also not shown satisfactory results, as the following indicates:

> "According to ISSER (Institute of Statistical Social and Economic Research), the outlook for Foreign Direct Investment on which our strategy relies is not very promising. From a peak of 474 million dollars in 1997, foreign direct investment was down to 58.9 million dollars last year." (Chronicle, Saturday, July 5, 2003: 3)

A recent study, which was carried on under the auspices of the Foreign Investment Advisory Service (FIAS, 2003) argued that Ghana's efforts to attract FDI have been be very poor. Ghana's average annual FDI inflows between 1997 and 2000 were a mere US$77.00 million. The average annual inflows of FDI were, in the same time period, into South Africa ($1.7 billion), Nigeria ($1.0 billion), Cote d'Ivoire ($338 million), Zambia ($172 million), Uganda ($171 million), Senegal ($100 million), and Mauritius ($95 million). Some plausible explanations for Ghana's poor performance, as the study highlights (FIAS 2003), can be (1) attributed, to some extent, the slowdown in the world economy and the slowdown in new international investment and (2) there is the possibility that the lack of interest from foreign investors results from the investment climate and the relatively high cost of doing business. The last point here, again, underlies the importance of having a marketing view as one competetes for FDI.

Some of Ghana's comparative advantages in the competition for FDI

As reported in Harrison (1993, p.357), 50 % of the manufacturing sales in Ghana in 1974 were accounted for by foreign enterprises. Lever Brothers Ghana (a subsidiary of Unilever) was regarded as one of the largest companies in terms of either capital investment or employment and industrial outputs for the domestic market and the export market (Roe, 1991; Awuah, 1994). The mining sector that became synonymous with FDI in recent times (Asante et al, 2000, p.34), with investors taking advantage of the government's incentive structure, became the country's largest foreign exchange earner, bringing cocoa to a second position. Shell Ghana, a foreign company that has been operating in Ghana for over 75 years, is said to pay 120 billion in duties, taxes and levies. It also contributes to the sustainable development of carefully selected causes in the areas of education, health and the environment (Chronicle, Monday June 30, 2003:5; Daily Graphic, Monday, July 21, 2003:28).

The presence of the foreign firms is an advantage in itself; the attitude towards foreign multinationals is positive. There are other advantages too. Ghana is famous for its production and sale of cocoa, timber, and minerals (gold, diamond, bauxite, and manganese). The present state of selling most of the above products on the world market as raw products could be an opportunity for investors that can process such products for several uses. The country also abounds in cotton, floriculture, lakes, rivers and the sea, most of which have various kinds of fish and/or seafood (Asante et al, 2000). They could all provide viable processing industries. Other products that could be processed are coffee, palm products and tropical fruits, products which are all abundant in their raw form in Ghana.

Ghana's services sector, such as trade, transport, communication, finance, hospitality industry (tourism, hotels, and restaurants), are also potential areas for investment. The Ghana Investment Promotion Centre (GIPC) that has been established to help guide investors to invest in Ghana is a positive thing, quite an advantage. It is also an advantage that Ghana now has a Free Zones Board which also helps and guides potential investors in their efforts to exploit the opportunities that Ghana offers. The country's democratic government and its Multilateral

Investment Guarantee Agreement can be seen as an advantage because it helps to create confidence in the investment climate in Ghana (Financial Times, July 11, 1989:3; Ghana Information Service Department's Publication, July, 1985; Asante et al, 2000; FIAS, 2003). Labour costs are low (FIAS, 2003).

Ghana's geographical and/or strategic position is an advantage in itself. The country is a member of the Economic Community of West African States (ECOWAS), a larger market that substitutes for the small market of Ghana. ECOWAS is about to adopt a common regional currency by the year 2007 (The Statesman, Monday July 21, 2003:4). Ghana's proximity to the main EU markets, with flights to London and Amsterdam averaging only six hours is seen as a comparative advantage.

Some weaknesses impacting on Ghana's search for FDI

Lack of reliable industrial infrastructure, limited markets, scarcity of locally-produced inputs, high cost of imported producer goods and difficult access to bank loans are some of the reasons for why many developing countries, such as Ghana, (IMF Report, 1985; Harrison, 1993, FIAS, 2003) are not able to attract many FDI. Even the presence of FDI cannot produce the desired effect as shown below.

> "One of the main reasons some recipient countries have suffered a negative balance of payments or decline in their trade surplus is that not enough parts and components companies have invested in them. Big manufacturers have to import parts, offsetting the trade surplus expected to follow FDI." (Financial Times, Friday, August 1, 2003:13).

As reported in the FIAS (2003) study, a range of factors, such as high interest rates, bank loan regulations and tax rates – the so called administrative barriers to investment -- impede the respondents' activities and cost of doing business. In sum, the report states as follows:

> "These issues all negatively affect the cost of doing business in Ghana and result from the poor design or

> implementation of laws and regulations and the delivery of services to the business community" (FIAS, 2003: Vi).

Ghana's track record, as far as stability in governments and government attitude towards private investment are concerned, has not been good. State controls of all important aspects of business and even harassment of businesspeople have been a feature of Ghana's business climate in the past (Panford, 1994, p. 80; Tangari, 1992, pp.100-101). Certainly, attempts to improve upon such an image could take a long time before potential investors would regain confidence in Ghana (Asante et al., 2000; Kuada and Sorensen, 2001). We can now draw some conclusions regarding why Ghana has not been completely successful in attracting FDI.

Conclusion

Certainly, Ghana has invested much effort and/or resources to attract and sustain FDI, as evident from the accounts given of the country's efforts in the late 1950s until the present time, the 21st century. However, why and how Ghana has been attracting and supporting FDI suggest that the country has had "double standards" regarding its promises to investors. While investors, at some periods in time, would be given incentives and protection from competition, the country has also been accused of massive intervention by the state in the conduct of business to the extent that businesses could not expand and new ones were scared away. In recent times the country seems to be working hard to regain the confidence, once lost from the potential and current investors, by not only signing bilateral and multilateral agreements to assure investors that the country would fulfill its promises regarding guarantees, incentives and protection of life and property, but it has also embarked on massive deregulating measures.

The established Ghana Investment Promotion Centre and Free Zones Board are all investments that should help win FDI into Ghana. The country's abundant natural resources, its strategic position within the ECOWAS, its friendly people, low costs and availability of labour along with political stability should be seen as a comparative advantage. Yet the FDI inflow has been quite disappointing. This poor result of winning and sustaining FDI has been a feature that the country has not been able to overcome. Ghana stands to gain by working hard to achieve sustainable comparative advantages, while doing all it can to overcome its weaknesses. All this makes us suggest that there is the need for empirical studies that might help us understand the extent to which Ghana has invested in attracting FDI and whether or not the efforts have failed to produce many positive results, as this paper currently reveals.

Further research

As reported in Swee, FDI are not only welcome, but actively sought after. Each government in the ASEAN region is said to have maintained expensive investment promotion offices in the major cities of industrial nations, posting some of the best talents to the offices.

"Governments would not do such things if they had any reservations about that value of foreign investment and the important role MNCs could play in the development of their economies" (Swee, G.K., 1995, p.117).

Research question (1)

In Ghana FDI seems to have flowed into the mining sector more than any other area in recent times (Asante et al, 2000). Can the knowledge gained about why and how FID flow into the mining sector be transferred to areas such as the agricultural and agro-processing sectors and the manufacturing sectors, where the likelihood of generating more employment, for example, is high?

Research question (2)

Should not Ghana start to do more target marketing by actively going after potential investors, which are best needed in some strategic areas in the economy, instead of going after every potential investor? How actively and effectively is Ghana marketing itself in some major cities of industrial countries, as some countries have done (see above)? This marketing approach is something which the existing theories (e.g. the eclectic theory of FDI) do not say anything about.

"One of the main reasons some recipient countries have suffered a negative balance of payments or decline in their trade surplus is that not enough parts and components companies have invested in them. Big manufacturers have to import parts, offsetting the trade surplus expected to follow FDI" (Financial Times, August 1, 2003: 13).

Targeting some parts and components companies from the industrial nations, for instance, to come and invest in Ghana is 'food for thought'. And what needs to be put into such an effort is the knowledge, shared in our theoretical part, that firms will undertake FDI to exploit, among other things, their firm-specific advantages under favourable and/or enabling environment (Kuada and Sorensen, 2001), which is far superior to other competing environments, including the firm's own domestic environment.

References

Alderson, W., (1957). *Marketing Behaviour and Executive Action: A Functionalist Approach to Marketing Theory*, Richard. D. Irwin, Homewood, IL.

Armstrong, G., Kotler, P., Saunders, J., and Wong, V, (2002). *Principles of Marketing*, Pearson Education Limited, Edinburgh Gate, Harlow.

Asante, Y., Gyasi, E.M., and Tsikata, G.K, (2000). *Determinants of Foreign Direct Investment in Ghana*, Overseas Development Institute, Portland House, Stage Place, London SW1E 5DP.

Asiedu, E., (2001). On the Determinants of Foreign Direct Investment to Developing Countries: Is Africa Different? *World Development* Vol. 30, No. 1, pp. 107-119.

Awuah, G.B., (1994). *The Presence of Multinational Companies (MNCs) in Ghana: A Study of the Impact of the Interaction between an MNC and Three Indigenous Companies*, Dissertation, Uppsala University, Uppsala.

Business & Financial Times, November 13-November 30, 1991:8

Business & Financial Times, January 27-February 9, 1994:4

Caves, R.E., (1982). *Multinational Enterprise and Economic Analysis*, Cambridge Press University.

Dagens Industri, Wednesday, May 5, 2004:15

Dagens Industri, Wednesday, October 20, 2004:17

Dagens Nyheter, November 9, 1992

Daily Graphic, Monday, July 21, 2003:28

Daniels and Radebaugh, (2001). *International Business: Environments and Operations,* 9th Edition, Prentice-Hall, London.

Dunning, J., (1981). *International Production and the Multinational Enterprise*, Allen & Unwin, London.

Dunning, J. (1993). *Multinational Enterprises and the Global Economy*, Addison-Wesley, Wokingham.

Economist, September 10-16, 1994:124

Economist, June 20, 2001:42

Economic Digest, January 22-28, 1990:3

Eriksson, G.A., (1990). *Development of the African Economy by Foreign Direct Investments with Special Reference to Nigeria*, Åbo-Akademis, Åbo.

FIAS (2003), *Ghana: Administrative Barriers to Investment Update*, Accra.

Fieldhouse, D.K., (1978). *"Unilever Overseas" – The Anatomy of a Multinational*, 1895-1965, Croom-Helm, London.

Financial Times, Friday, August 1, 2003:13

Financial Times, July 11, 1989:3

Garlick, P.C., (1971). *African Traders and Economic Development in Ghana*, Clarendon Press, Oxford, London.

Ghana Drum, November, 1993:30-31

Ghana Exporters' Directory, (1991). Worldwide Press Limited, Accra.

Ghana: *Handbook of Commerce and Industry*, (1988/89). Ministry of Trade and Tourism, Accra.

Ghana Information Service Department's Publication, July 13, 1985, Accra.

Ghana Today, June, 1994:26

GIPC (2004). Attracting FDI, available at: http://www.gipc.org.gh/Ipa_printinformation.asp, (accessed September 16, 2004)

Griffin, R., Mahoney, D., Pustay, M., Trigg, M, (1998). *International Business*, Longman, South Melbourne, Australia.

Harrison, P., (1993). *Inside the Third World: The Anatomy of Poverty*, 3rd Edition, England.

Hennart, J-F., (1982). *Economic Theories of Multinational Enterprises*, Ann Arbor.

Hollensen, S., (2001). *Global Marketing: Marketing-responsive Approach*, 2nd Edition, Prentice-Hall, Essex.

International Monetary Fund (IMF)-Report, (1985). *Foreign Private Investment in Developing Countries*, Washington D.C.

Johanson, J. & Associates, (1994). *Internationalization, Relationships and Networks,* Acta Universitatis Upsaliensis. Studia Oecenomiae Negotiorum, 36, Uppsala University, Sweden.

Killick, T., (1981). *Policy Economics: A Textbook of Applied Economics on Developing Countries*, Heineman, London.

Kuada, J and Sorensen, O.J., (2001). Firms in the South: Interactions between National Business Systems and the Global Economy. In: Jakobsen, G and Torp, J.E (Editors), *Understanding Business Systems in Developing Countries*, Sage Publications, New Delhi/London.

Newsweek, June, 1992:27

Panford, K., (1994). Structural Adjustment, the State and Workers in Ghana: An African Development, *Quarterly Journal of the Council for the Development of Social Science Research*, Codesria, Dakar.

Reuber, G.L., (1973). Private Foreign Investment in Development, Oxford University Press, London, W.1.

Roe, A.R., (1991). *Economy*. In Regional Survey of the World: Africa South of Sahara (1992), 21st edition, Europe Publications Limited, London.

Swee, G.K., (1995). *Wealth of East Asian Nations*, Federal Publications Pte. Limited, Singapore.

Tangari, R., (1992). The Politics of Government –Business Relations in Ghana. *The Journal of Modern African Studies* 30, 97-111.

Teece, D., (1985). Transaction Cost Economics and the Multinational Enterprise. An Assessment, Journal of Economic Behaviours and Organisation, 7, pp.21-45.

Todaro, M.P., (1994). *Economic Development*, 5th Edition, Longman Publishing, New York.

The Chronicle, Saturday, July 5, 2003:3

The Chronicle, Monday, June 30, 2003:5

The Statesman, Wednesday, July 2, 2003:6

United Nations Report, 1978:237

West Africa, August 1-7, 1994:1350

Williams, D.A., Wint, A. G., (2002). Attracting FDI to Developing Countries. A Changing Role for Governments? *The International Journal of Public Sector Management*, Vol. 15 No. 5, pp. 361-374.

World Development Report, (1994). *Infrastructure for Development*. Published for the World Bank, Oxford University Press, Oxford/New York/Toronto.

World Development Report (1990). *Poverty,* Published for the World Bank, Oxford University Press, Oxford/new York/Toronto.

Chapter Five

Foreign Loans And Development Help In A Country's Economic Development Process

The controversy on foreign loans and development help (or aid)

> "Little or no evidence has been found to indicate that the transfer of technology and skills via foreign direct investment and training afforded by such investment are substitutes for local development of technology and skills and for local training. In general, a complementary relationship seems more likely…As pointed above, the effects of a foreign investment appear to be complementary with many aspects of local development. Thus, the infant-industry argument in this context is not a matter of deciding between substitutes but rather of shifting the degree of complementarity so that more local advantages are associated with given inputs of foreign direct investment" (Reuber, 1973, p. 244).

The controversy on foreign aid and development help becomes apparent when one analyzes numerous debates or discussions on them. For example, in February 1990, an international conference on Popular Participation in the Recovery and Development Process in Africa almost declared war against the International Monetary Fund (IMF) and the World Bank sponsored Structural Adjustments Programmes (SAP). The SAP, as the critics argue, worsens the economic situation of any country that embarks on their implementation. The economic situation of the recipient countries, which receive aid from foreign donors, does not get better as intended and expected by all. The following quotation adds to the controversy or the negative perception of foreign aid (loans or development aid with no obligation to pay back):

> "Foreign Aid comes with a fee-good factor. We can be satisfied that we are – our countries are – contributing to the economic well-being of starving people in the Third World. Even if only a small percentage of our money goes to that aid, at least we did something positive. Or did we?
>
> "…Zambian writer Evans Munyemesha does not think so. In an article International Aid, published in The Zambian, he charges that development aid, 'has financed the creation of monstrous projects that, at vast expense, have devastated the environment and ruined lives'. Rather than getting down to 'the hard task of worth creation', Munyemesha says, 'easy handouts' have been substituted 'for the rigors of self-help', leaving the receiving countries economically crippled and their people worse off than before. If we look at the results, African 'aid' has been an unlimited disaster:
>
> *"Africa has lost self-sufficiency in food production that it enjoyed before development assistance was invented, and during the past few decades, has become instead a continent-sized beggar hopelessly dependent on the largesse of outsiders—per-capita food production has fallen in every year since the 1960s. Seven out of every ten Africans, are now reckoned to be destitute or on the verge of extreme poverty, with the result that the continent has the highest infant mortality rates, the fewest doctors per head of population, and the fewest children in school" (New Media Explorer, 2007)."*
>
> ". . .Whenever such suggestions are made the lobbyists throw up their hands in horror and consternation. Despite some regrettable failures, they protest, 'aid is justifiable by its successes; despite some glitches and problems, it's

> essentially something that works; most important of all – the emotional touch, the appeal to the heartstrings--- they argue with passion that 'aid' must not be stopped because the poor could not survive without it.
>
> ". . .Such statements, however, patronize and undervalue the people of the poor countries concerned. They are, in addition, logically indefensible when uttered by those who also want us to believe that 'aid' works. Throughout history and pre-history all countries everywhere got by perfectly all right without any 'aid' at all. Furthermore, in the 1950s they got by with much less 'aid' than they did, for example, in the 1970s—and were apparently none the worse for the experience. Now, suddenly, at the tail end almost sixty years of development assistance, we are told that large numbers of the same countries have lost the ability to survive a moment longer unless they continue to receive ever-larger amounts of 'aid'. If this is indeed the case—and if the only measurable impact of all these decades of development has been to turn resolute and tenacious survivors into helpless dependents—then it seems to me to be beyond dispute that 'aid' does not work" (p.2 of 5 of the New Media Explorer).

Relating the above quotes from the Media Explorer to the first quote from Reuter (1973), the reader finds that seeing foreign aid (loans or just development help) as a substitute for the local developmental capacity building would be completely wrong. We need to see any foreign aid (e.g. loans, development help, or foreign direct investment) as a complement to the local or indigenous resources (human and non-human). The foreign aid and the indigenous resources complement each other; none of them can be a substitute for the other. One would, therefore, understand Munyemesha's (see above) worry about the negative result of the so called foreign aid to Africa. Foreign aids, which are supposed to have been brought into many African countries' development process to assist in the efficient and productive use of the countries' own indigenous resources, have not yielded the expected results (World Development Report, 1994; Spiegel Special, 2007).

> "…Let us take our minds back to 30 years ago. The Second World War had just ended. The losers, Germany, Japan and Italy lay prostrate. German and Japanese cities and industries had been razed to the ground by Allied bombing. The victors, except for the USA, were hardly in better shape.
>
> ". . .Both the victors and the vanquished worked hard to restore their economies. This called for immense capital investment – in the rebuilding of the cities, ports, railway systems; new factories, shipyards, steel mills had to be set up. Fortunately for mankind, the winners of World War II adopted an intelligent attitude towards the losers and did not repeat the mistake of the spiteful Treaty of Versailles.
>
> ". . .The American economy was the first to recover and was able to assist Europe through the Marshall Plan to rapid recovery. Marshall Plan aid and other forms of aid provided by the Americans yielded quick returns in Europe and Japan, unlike aid being supplied through various channels to Third World countries today. The reason was that Western Europe and Japan had the infrastructure of scientific, technical, management and organisational know-how and this enabled them to put loans and aid funds to effective use." (Swee, 1995, p. 62).

The above quote from Swee (1995) reinforces the thesis put forth here. Thus, foreign loans and aid funds are brought into the recipient country's development process to assist in the efficient and productive use of the country's own resources. Looking at what happened in the reconstruction of Western Europe and Japan after World War II, the proponents of the giving of aid and loans as an important impetus in a country's development should not be questioned. But, where the recipient country has no internal capacity to enable the country to be receptive and to efficiently use the foreign loan or aid funds as complementary to the country's own internal resources (human and non-human), we have the situation such as many countries in the Less Developed Countries (LDCs) find themselves. An important concern had/has been the dependence on foreign aids, in the form of loans (interest loaded and interest free loans). Foreign donors of aid to poor countries (especially the IMF and the World Bank) went to the extent of prescribing the conditions under which the loan a country took/takes should be utilized. Recipients of loans were told how to operate efficiently, from the perspective of the donors of aid, but not from that of the recipients (World Development Report, 1990, 1994). Yet, submitting to the dictates of the donor organisations or countries has not yielded the expected results or progress, for many LDCs. The recipients of the Marshall Plan aid were capable of deciding how and where they wanted to invest the aid.

Dependence on foreign loans and aid, a vicious circle

Ghana, like many countries in Africa, seems to have been caught up in the foreign loans and aids trap. As reported elsewhere (Fieldhouse, 1978, p. 412), the economic climate in Ghana had already deteriorated in the 1960s. The country was said to have suffered from an accelerated adverse balance of trade because of reduced cocoa prices and government massive spending. It is also reported that during the 1970s and early 1980s, Ghana's accumulated trade deficit almost paralyzed the economy (Roe, 1991, p. 509; Ghana: handbook of Commerce and Industry, 1988, P. 9). The need for foreign aid or loans and investment is said to date back to the 1950s and 1960s (e.g. Garlick, 1971; Roe, 1991). Especially in the 1980s, the Ghana government was compelled to call on several international organisations such as the IMF and the World Bank for help (Tangari, 1992; Akwetey, 1994; Panford, 1994). The loans or the help, which Ghana received from some foreign donors of loans, did not yield any positive result. As the state deficit grew very high, especially in the 1970s, Ghana was pushed into heavy borrowing. Akwetey (1994, p. 78) reports that Ghana's foreign debt grew from US $895 million in 1975 to US $1,429 million in 1979. This made international institutions decide to disqualify Ghana from receiving further loans or credits (p.78). If Ghana could receive further loans, it had to undertake some reforms, which the IMF and the World Bank recommended as a means to offer their support for loans from the respective institutions and even from other foreign organisations (Roe, 1991; World Development Report, 1994).

Once Ghana began to reform the economy, as advised by the World Bank and the IMF, going for loans from foreign institutions (e.g. IMF and The World Bank) became easy (Roe, 1991; Ghana Today, 1994:17). The World Bank even made Ghana in 1987, after China and India, its greatest recipient of interest free development loans (Svenska Dagbladet, January 18, 1989:4; Der Spiegel 35/1989:142). The massive foreign loans that Ghana again obtained, as the country embarked on the reforms suggested by the World Bank and the IMF, ought to have contributed to the development that should have made the country self-reliant and, for that matter, broken the 'vicious circle' of loan taking as the only means to develop.

The challenge here is that, at a certain point in time, foreign loans (interest loaded loans or interest free loans) will be pulled out of the country's development process. The country has to pay back its debt to the creditors. This is where stock is taken to ascertain what has come out of the use of the foreign loans. There are two main results which the indebted country and the creditors are bound to see. These are positive and negative results. In the case of Ghana, the positive result could be that the country is able to pay its debts and is able to continue its positive development, having a sustainable development, while foreign debts have been paid. Unfortunately, in Ghana the result of having massive foreign loans has been negative. Ghana is, in the millennium, classified as one of the highly indebted poor countries in the world. The government had to apply and be admitted into the Highly Indebted Poor Countries (HIPC) Initiative. This initiative, as declared by the current president, Kuffour, has enabled Ghana to enjoy 7 billion dollars debt cancellation (Development Debate, 2007).

Ghana's plight discussed above seems to convey the idea that there is no other solution to the economic crisis in the country except the inflow of foreign loans or aid. The dilemma is that loans taken are not paid back because the country does not have the capacity to do so. A long term consequence of this predicament would be the reluctance of foreign institutions to offer loans to Ghana again. The quotation below says it all:

> "...But the U.S. has resisted a British proposal for wealthy nations to service World Bank debt on behalf of

> poorer countries, and President Bush is not on pace to fulfil his 2003 pledge of $15 billion in development aid to Africa. Further, while the U.S. is the largest contributor in international development aid in total dollars, it devotes the lowest percentage of gross national income in foreign aid of the 22 rich countries that make the Development Assistance Committee (DAC) of the Organisation for Economic Co-operation and Development (OECD).
>
> ". . .The United States has opposed a plan by British Chancellor of the Exchequer Gordon Brown in which wealthy nations would pay off the debt that poor nations owe to the World Bank. The United States favors a less generous proposal in which the World Bank would simply write off Third World debts, rather than having rich countries take them over. In return, poor countries would accept lower aid levels in the future" (Media Matters).

If Ghana and many other African countries do not look into their own internal capacity building, instead of being caught in the 'vicious circle' of receiving foreign aid and loans as a means to develop their respective economies, the time is almost nigh that no such thing would happen. The U.S. is suggesting, as the above quote indicates, that poor countries would have to accept lower aid levels in the future. As for giving loans to a poor country in the future, who would do that, knowing very well that the recipient would not be able to pay back the loan? At any rate private loan givers, managing shareholders' monetary assets, would not invest in anything where they are not sure of a positive return on the investment. And for many countries in Africa, they know for sure that the countries are not credit worthy. Should poor countries such as Ghana and others in Africa bank all their hopes, in the effort to raise the living standards of their people, on foreign loans and aid? The answer is simply no. As argued earlier, foreign loans or aid to poor countries, should, in the future, be like the Marshall Plan that Western Europe and Japan enjoyed. They would no longer be forthcoming; United States of America is sounding the warning already, as can be seen in the above quote. Ghana, for example, needs to break free from its total dependence on foreign loans and aid and turn to its own internal resource (human and non-human) development.

Breaking free from the grips of foreign aid and loans, away with the vicious cycle

Foreign loans and aid, when available, should not be rejected. But, it has to be reiterated that they are brought into a country's development process to assist in the efficient and productive use of the country's own resources. Much will depend upon the extent to which the indigenous resources are prepared to meet and take advantage of the external resources (loans and aid). That foreign loans and aid are a complement to a country's indigenous resources should raise the awareness of poor nations concerning the importance to prepare the indigenous resources, especially the human aspect, which complement the external resources that flow into a country.

For Ghana, it is about time the country built action groups, irrespective of political views held by the members of such groups to tackle some defined problems facing the society as a whole. For example, since the 1950s until today, 2007, Ghana has not been able to guarantee its citizens a 24 hour supply of electricity and pipe-borne water. The industrial shut-downs and the closure of other activities in the society, as the result of the electricity power failure and lack of water, are a major setback in the country's development. These two items, electricity and water, are the lifeblood of modern civilisation; individuals and organisations/firms, in the modern and globalize world, would function sub-optimally, to say the least, if they have irregular access to electricity and water. The Volta Aluminium Company (Valco), one of the largest companies in terms of all measurements (sheer size, turnover, employees and its role as a supplier of raw materials to many firms), currently, at the time of writing this book, operates at 30 % below capacity because of the lack of electricity. Isn't that a waste of resources (both human and non-human)? When will the authorities realize the scenario(s) that the country needs to expand its capacity in supplying adequate and regular electricity to all and sundry in the society? A lot of things are in bad shape, not only electricity and water supply.

However, going back to the advice being advanced here, we need action groups that transcend all interest groups. The action groups, composed of people with varied backgrounds, competencies, and experiences, would be scanning the environment, looking at trends, changes in all spheres of life that might have an impact on the society, and build scenarios to pinpoint threats and opportunities, which stem from the trends and changes. They would then suggest possible measures to ward off threats, while suggesting measures to explore the emerged opportunities. There should be proper and efficient infrastructure to support the action groups. And there should be receptive institutions (with the decision makers working in them) that would interact with the action groups so that, together, the actors can effectively tackle the numerous problems facing the country. There should be a vehement search for local people who possess various skills and resources needed to take advantage of, for example, external resources that might flow into the country. Or dwelling on their own skills and competencies, the local people might see the strength in co-operating with each other to solve some defined problems of national interest. Ghana's history has it that the first president of Ghana, Dr. Kwame Nkrumah, was actively sought after by fellow Ghanaians and they even financed his return to Ghana after his 19 year stay in the Diaspora (in the U.S. and England respectively). In the 1970s, many Ghanaians had to leave Ghana for the Diaspora because of the hardships they faced in Ghana (Awuah, 2005; Adjei, 1994).

In the 1980s, however, many people that had gone to live in the Diaspora returned home, some willingly and some forcibly (Awuah, 2005). The many Ghanaian returnees from the Diaspora brought with them various skills and resources and, hence, decided to invest in Ghana. Since there was/is no purposeful effort, on the part of the policy makers particularly and the general public in general, many of the Ghanaian returnees from the Diaspora lost both their hard won resources and the motivation and the courage to stay on in Ghana. Many of them were subjected to all sorts of unfavourable conditions such as bureaucratic hindrances, discrimination, robbery and deceits. Instead of being helped to re-integrate into the Ghanaian society, many of them had to 'run away' from Ghana into the Diaspora again.

So those who cry for certain Ghanaians in the Diaspora to just pack their things and come home might think about what it is that is preventing some Ghanaians from returning home. Putting oneself in the shoes of a fellow Ghanaian might be worthwhile; it is a sign that one cares about the interests and problems of a fellow countryperson. It can be and probably, is true that the limitations in Africa in general, and in Ghana in particular, might not lie so much on physical things like lack of foreign loans and aid, but probably on the lack of empathy and co-operation among the people.

The current Ministry of Diaspora is a positive thing. It is a sign that efforts are being made to welcome and help people from the Diaspora to come home to Ghana and help develop the country. Hopefully, the national effort being made here is not targeting only African Americans, but also Ghanaians, who had once lived in the Diaspora but want to return home. Anybody from the Diaspora, a Ghanaian or an African American or other people of African descent, should be seen and treated as potential capable of helping to 'inject' resources (e.g. knowledge, information and physical capital) into the development process set in motion in Ghana.

This is not to say that the country should not be vigilant concerning unscrupulous elements that might, through self-seeking interest and with guile, use the Diaspora gesture now in place in the country to enter Ghana and commit crimes. For example, entering the country to deal in drug trafficking and other vices, which are detrimental to development, should not be encouraged. As said before, there should be a genuine effort to search among Ghanaians, both at home and in the Diaspora, to help and support those who want to do something for Ghana. Many of the challenges facing all in Ghana and most parts of the world would demand collective solutions instead of individual efforts.

We will finish this chapter with some famous quotations which underline the power of joining forces. The first quotation is about Mr. Kroc, the man who helped grow the McDonalds' Empire and Walt Disney. The second quotation is from Mr. Nelson Mandela.

> "Kroc and Disney both dropped out of high school and later added the trappings of formal education to their companies… They were charismatic figures who provided an overall corporate vision and grasped the public mood, relying on others to handle the creative and financial details. Walt Disney neither wrote, nor drew the animated classics that bore his name" (Schlosser, E., 2002p.33).

> "A nation should not be judged by how it treats its highest citizens, but its lowest ones – and South Africa treated its imprisoned African citizens like animals" (Mandela, N. R, 1994, p. 233).

> " Suddenly there were no Xhosas or Zulus, no Indians or Africans, no rightists or leftists, no religious or political leaders; we were all nationalists and patriots bound together by a love of our common history, our culture, our country and our people. In that moment, something stirred deep inside all of us, something strong and intimate that bound us to one another. In that moment we felt the hand of the great past that made us what we were and the power of the great cause that linked us all together" (Mandela, N. R, 1994, p. 235).

The above quotes show the relative importance of collective efforts in the accomplishment of set goals.

Summary

In summary, the foreign loans and aid which a country receives can be of a tremendous help, if and only if, they are seen as complementary to the recipient country's own internal resources. Foreign loans and aid should not be seen as substitutes for the recipient country's own internal resources. The Marshall Plan aid assistance for the reconstruction of Western Europe and Japan after the World War II did not continue forever. The donor country, U.S.A., discontinued giving the aid because the recipient countries knew how to combine the foreign aid and their own internal capacity, which enabled them to effectively develop further their own economies, an effort which in the long run enabled the countries to eliminate their reliance on the Marshall Plan aid. Ghana, in particular, and many African and other poor countries in general, have not been able to eliminate or reduce the dominance of foreign loans and aid in the efforts to bring about socio-economic development. One important thesis put forward in this chapter is that Ghana would have to prepare its indigenous resources (human and non-human) to meet and take advantage of external resources, in varied forms, which might flow into the country.

The long term goal for Ghana would be to break free from the vicious circle of 'loan taking', which has placed the country into the Highly Indebted Poor Countries (HIPC) Initiative category. This throws a real challenge for Ghana to search vehemently within its indigenous resources (both human and non-human) and encourage the development of its entrepreneurial base. The entrepreneurial base is said to be lacking in many countries in Africa (Caves, 1982; Unger, 1988). This brings us to discuss the need for Ghana to encourage and support the development of the country's entrepreneurial base.

References

Adjei, M. (1994). *Death and Pain: Rawlings' Ghana – The Inside Story*, London. Black Line Publishing Ltd.

Akwetey, E. (1994). *Trade Unions and Democratization: A Comprehensive Study of Zambia and Ghana*, Dissertation, Department of Political Science, University of Stockholm, Stockholm.

Awuah, G, B. (2005). *As I Journey Along: A Ghanaian's Perception of Life in the Diaspora*, U.S.A. Lulu Press.

Caves, R.E., (1982). *Multinational Enterprise and Economic Analysis*, Cambridge Press University.

Der Spiegel 35/1989:142

Development Debate (2007), Debate on some development paths taken in Ghana, available at: http://www.ghanaweb.com/GhanaHomePage/NewsArchives/artikel.php?ID=119493: (Accessed, February 2, 2007).

Fieldhouse, D.K. (1978). *"Unilever Overseas" – The Anatomy of a Multinational*, 1895-1965, London , Croom-Helm.

Ghana: *Handbook of Commerce and Industry*, (1988/89). Ministry of Trade and Tourism, Accra.

Ghana Today, June 1994: 17-24

Mandela, N, R. (1994). *Long Walk to Freedom*. Great Britain. By Little, Brown and Company.

Media Maters (2007). Report on Aid to Poor Countries, available at: http://www.mediamatters.org/items: (accessed 27-03-2007)

New Media Explorer (2007), Report on International Aid, available at: http://www.newmediaexplorer.org/sepp: (accessed 27-03-2007).

Panford, K. (1994). Structural Adjustment, the State and Workers in Ghana: An African Development, *Quarterly Journal of the Council for the Development of Social Science Research*, Codesria, Dakar.

Reuber, G.L., (1973). Private Foreign Investment in Development, London, W.1. Oxford University Press.

Roe, A.R. (1991). *Economy*. In Regional Survey of the World: Africa South of Sahara (1992), (21st Ed.). London, Europe Publications Limited.

Schlosser, E. (2002). *Fast Food Nation: What the All American is Doing to the World*. London. Penguin Books Ltd.

Svenska Dagbladet, January 18, 1989:4

Swee, G.K., (1995). *Wealth of East Asian Nations*, Singapore Federal Publications Pte. Limited.

Tangari, R. (1992). The Politics of Government –Business Relations in Ghana. *The Journal of Modern African Studies* 30, 97-111

Unger, K. (1988). Industrial Structure, Technical Change and Micro-economic Behaviour in LDCs. In Dosi et al (ed.). (1988). *Technical Change and Economic Theory*. London. Pinter Publishers.

World Development Report, (1994). *Infrastructure for Development*. Published for the World Bank, Oxford University Press, Oxford/New York/Toronto.

World Development Report (1990). *Poverty,* Published for the World Bank, Oxford University Press, Oxford/New York/Toronto.

Chapter Six

The Need For Ghana To Encourage And Support Entrepreneurial Base Development

Relationship between effective entrepreneurial base and economic development

One of the central issues of development which economists discuss about effective economic development in a country has to do with the efforts made by entrepreneurs. As argued by Caves (1982, pp. 270-271), the input-output relationships between entrepreneurs create linkage effects. Backward linkages are created in an economy when a firm purchases its production inputs from other firms or suppliers. Forward linkages have to do with a firm supplying its outputs, which become inputs to other processes and activities. Caves (1982) puts it categorically that many cells in the input-output table of a developing country are empty because of lack of entrepreneurial efforts or other forces (p. 271). Hence, for an effective development, there is the need for encouraging specific demand for outputs or concrete supply of inputs, which will provoke viable activities in an economy.

Relating the above discussions to the situation facing Ghana, the lack of the entrepreneurial base in Ghana becomes very obvious when one considers the on-going debates in the country in recent times. The following quotation is a case in point:

> "Ghana has not been able to change the structure of its economy for over 40 years as the country still relies on the export of raw materials and also depends mostly on

> foreign donors and her development partners to fund development budgets.
>
> It is unacceptable that about 80 per cent of inputs into agriculture, education and health are from foreign sources" (Development Debate, 2007).

Submitting to Caves (1982), Ghana will need to encourage and support entrepreneurs within the country that will help fill the cells in the input-output table, which are very empty. The linkages from the input-output relationships would, among other things, reduce many sectors' reliance on foreign inputs, which are also a major drain on the country's balance of trade or balance of payment. For years Ghana has suffered a negative balance of payments because many sectors, manufacturing, agriculture, health and education (Roe, 1991; World Development Report, 1990, 1994), rely heavily on foreign production inputs.

Who is an entrepreneur?

In Caves' (1982) terminology, as the above discussions show, an entrepreneur is a firm that engages in undertaking business ventures. The entrepreneur or the firm might be a supplier of inputs to other firms, creating in that act forward linkages in the economy. The firm can also buy other firms' output, to be used in its production processes or other transformation activities, thereby creating, with that act backward linkages in an economy. Notably, a firm can be owned and run by a single individual. A firm can also be owned and run by several individuals or a corporation. What they all have in common is that they create and establish exchange relationships among themselves, since one's output becomes another's input. So an economy where there are many suppliers of inputs because demand is encouraged would produce viable activity for the entrepreneurs. Analogously, where the outputs of firms are absorbed because there are markets for them, entrepreneurs delivering those outputs are encouraged to go on with their activities. The absence of production inputs, as Ghana's situation portrays, would discourage entrepreneurs to emerge and exploit whatever market opportunities they envisage. Similarly, the absence of markets for locally produced goods and services in an economy would also discourage entrepreneurs to risk investing.

For some writers, however, an entrepreneur is seen as an individual who is alert to profitable opportunities and exchange because of imperfect knowledge (Deakins, 1999). According to Schumpeter (1934), an entrepreneur is a special person, an innovator, who is capable of introducing viable activities through innovation, where new technological processes or products are used. In the 1930s, Schumpeter (1934) launched his concept of entrepreneurial action, which today still has much relevance (Andersson, 2000). Schumpeter's (1934, p. 66) entrepreneurial concepts comprised not only the introduction of new products, but also the introduction of new production methods, opening of new markets, conquests of new sources of supply and raw materials, and the running of a new organization in an industry. Most importantly, entrepreneurial action and/or drive result in the founding of a company to exploit the envisaged opportunities. As argued by Storey (1996), a company can be either established by an individual or by a group of individuals, called entrepreneurial teams. With an entrepreneurial team, a company has different and important human resources from the very beginning, which makes it important to draw on varied skills (such as marketing knowledge and technology) that will facilitate the company's growth and success.

An entrepreneur needs to operate in an enabling environment

Whether we focus on an entrepreneur as an individual or as a firm, owned either by an individual or a team, one important thing to bear in mind is that the entrepreneurs' role in the input-output relationship should be seen as indispensable. This is because entrepreneurs do not only see the opportunities in the marketplace, they take risks. Entrepreneurs are also aware of the knowledge imperfection they possess and the general uncertainties which their decisions (e.g. market uncertainties, technology uncertainties and demand uncertainties) might result in (Porter, 1998; Deakins, 1999; Delmar, 1996). No matter how one sees an entrepreneur, an individual or a firm, the entrepreneur will invest where there is the opportunity for profit. If Ghana, for example, wants a potential entrepreneurial base to be developed, whereby many entrepreneurs dare to take risks and invest, an enabling environment (with abundant opportunities) needs to be created. The enabling environment lacking in Ghana has been pointed out elsewhere (Awuah,

1994; Asante et al, 2000; Kuada and Sorensen, 2001; FIAS, 2003). Ghana's problems, such as the lack of reliable industrial infrastructure, scarcity of locally-produced inputs, high cost of imported producer goods and services, irregular supply of electricity and water, and difficult access to bank loans (FIAS, 2003), do not present an enabling environment for entrepreneurs.

What needs to be kept in mind is that entrepreneurs can emerge from everywhere, the poorest or richest sections in the society, if there is an enabling environment. The following illustrates this point:

> "Entrepreneurs from all over the country went to San Bernardino, visited the new McDonald's and built imitations of the restaurant in their hometowns. 'Our food was exactly the same as McDonald's,' the founder of a rival chain later admitted. If I had looked at McDonald's and saw someone flipping hamburgers while he was hanging by his feet, I would have copied it'. America's fast food chains were not launched by large corporations relying upon focus groups and market research. They were started by door-to-door salesmen, short-order cooks, orphans, and dropouts, by eternal optimists looking for a piece of the next big thing. The start-up costs of a fast food restaurant were low, the profit margins promised to be high, and a wide assortment of ambitious people were soon buying grills and putting up signs" (Schlosser, 2002, p. 22).

Schlosser (2002, p. 22) states further how the founders of many famous fast food restaurants (e.g. Dunkin' Donuts, Taco Bell, and Insta-Burger King) copied McDonald's and established their own successful companies. When the McDonald's company introduced the assembly-line system to make its food, many fast food restaurants copied that too. All this shows that entrepreneurs can emerge not only from many areas but they tend to copy and spread successful concepts and/or practices, thereby evoking viable activities in an economy. Similar entrepreneurial behaviour, a successful business idea, or practice copied by many others is not a country-specific phenomenon. It happens in Ghana and many other countries too. In Ghana successful entrepreneurs have had tremendous impact on the copying and diffusion of their businesses, bringing similar activities into many parts of the country. The only difference is that in Ghana the entrepreneurs that emerge, after copying or coming up with some successful business practices, are not able to build the critical business platforms which will enable them survive when competition intensifies. Ghana is accused of lacking the enabling environment (FIAS, 2003; Kuada and Sorensen, 2001) which will enable entrepreneurs emerge and grow.

If Ghana could encourage and support entrepreneurs to invest in producing parts, components and some industrial raw materials, for example, in the country, there is the likelihood that their success would attract other potential entrepreneurs, as the above example of McDonald's shows. To this end, shouldn't Ghana encourage and support better collaboration between universities, other areas of higher learning and the industries? Shouldn't Ghana use sound fiscal and monetary policies to help and protect local industries? Let us consider a mini case that warrants encouragement of collaboration between several actors in an economy that faces intense foreign competition, the toughest challenge of globalization.

Mini Case 1

A Ghanaian entrepreneur, a resident in the US, had spotted business opportunities in Ghana, and was driven by those strategic windows that seemed to have been lying open, to come to Ghana to invest in a number of businesses. This entrepreneur's businesses spanned across several industries. The entrepreneur in question is the managing director of the Shasha group of companies. Shasha's portfolio of businesses are as follows: (1) A nail producing factory, (2) Motor tyre repair services, helping drivers to fix their 'flat' tyres in no time, (3) Retailing of fashionable clothes, (4) A photo studio, where people can be photographed at the studio or at whatever venue chosen by the customer, and (5) The buying and selling of hard wares (here, building materials). In terms of Ghanaian business standards, the managing director has invested millions of cedis in those diversified businesses, 1, 2, 3, 4, and 5. In the remainder of this chapter we will refer to this entrepreneur as the managing director of Shasha.

The first time that I met the managing director of Shasha, in July 2003, he took me around to show me all his businesses. Business 5 was a later investment; it was not in the managing director's business portfolio then. During our tour of the businesses in 2003, I could see a real joy and contentment in this managing director as we visited each of the first four businesses in turn. The various businesses seemed to be yielding some satisfactory positive results, especially the nail business, Business 1, which was the core business of this energetic managing director. Apparently, the business climate in Ghana had been very conducive for this managing director to dare to invest in such diversified industries. In July 2003 this business man had a number of positive things to say about the business climate.

Among his businesses, the managing director considered the manufacturing of nails to be the core business area of the Shasha group of companies. According to the managing director, there were times that the nail factory produced well over 90 % of its capacity. In product terms, the factory made over 20 tons finished nails a month. The market could absorb the products, which were sold at about 110 old Ghanaian cedis per carton, which weighed about 2.5 kilograms. During such times, the factory engaged the services of six permanent employees plus a number of part-time workers who were hired every day to help meet delivery deadlines. None of the other businesses matched the nail business in terms of revenue and employment generation. The rest of the four businesses employed, at most, a single person each to man the business at all times. Hence, we will focus on the nail factory in the rest of this chapter, as we try to analysis the problems encountered by a Ghanaian entrepreneur such as the one we are considering here.

In 2003, the Shasha nail factory was equipped with two heavy nail producing machines, each producing different sizes of nails. There was also a machine that made the final "polishing" and/or quality control before the finished nails were put in some locally purchased cartons, ready for delivery to buyers. Some buyers might drive in to take their purchases, while many others would have their purchases delivered to them by Shasha in its own vehicle. In 2005, because the demand for its nails was increasing, the managing director of the factory decided to expand the production capacity by buying an additional nail producing machine from India, the supply source of the machines to the company.When I re-visited the Shasha nail company in 2005, at midsummer, I met only four dismayed workers. A chat with the workers revealed that they were facing a tremendous problem. One of the two nail-producing machines was almost out of service; it needed to be serviced, which would demand the purchase of spare parts. Since these parts are all imported by distributors or retailers, the prices at which they are sold to users that need them are very high. They had very little money to buy spare parts, pay the workers, and cover other important costs (raw materials and overhead costs). These problems were attributed to the influx of nails into Ghana by Chinese and Indian exporters, which had caused buyers of locally made nails to switch to imported ones. The question is why are the local manufacturers of nails not able to compete with the influx of foreign competitors that now sell nails in Ghana? The answer(s) to this was sought from the owner, managing director of Shasha, the nail company under study.

On September 30, 2007, I engaged the managing director of the Shasha Company in a two and a half hour telephone interview at his residence in New Jersey, U.S.A. I wanted to welcome him back to the U. S., since he had been in Ghana for over four months to oversee his businesses, and also to interview him about the condition of his nail business. This longitudinal approach was appropriate because it enabled me to find out, from the managing director, what has been going on with the Shasha Company's performance over time, especially considering the intense competition that had emerged in the marketplace. I was trying to cross-check the information that his workers had told me during my 2005 visit to his nail factory. The managing director was more than delighted to answer any questions I had about his business and even to supply additional information that he thought was worthwhile, in particular, and the business climate in Ghana, in general. At the time of the telephone interview, the managing director sounded very pessimistic and disparate. His first statement sounded as follows: "Doc., if the business conditions facing us, and all nail producing companies in Ghana, continue as they are now, I will have to close my nail business next year." His nail business was started seven years ago, reckoned from the time of the telephone interview on September 30, 2007. According to the managing director, even some big competitors, such as Sahara, also a local producer have already closed down. The problems facing all local manufacturers of nails were narrated as follows by the managing director of Shasha.

In Kumasi, where the managing director has his nail factory, there are about 6 other big local manufacturers of nails. The number of local producers can be about 20, spread throughout Ghana. Therefore there is an intense competition between the local producers of nails in the country already. What all the local producers have in common, according to the managing director, is summarized as follows:

> They are all dependent on the importation of essential production inputs. Examples are heavy machines for producing nails, spare parts, lubricants to maintain the machines, and raw materials (nails wires). These are bought from distributors in Ghana who, in turn, import the items from overseas markets. The original producers of those essential production inputs will price their goods to cover their essential costs and with reasonable profit margins before their distributors in Ghana also price the goods to cover their costs and to reap some reasonable margins too. As a result, the local producers of nails will buy production inputs, most of which are imported, at some high prices.

The managing director continues his story:

> The Shasha Company, and other nail producers in Ghana, will pay higher prices for the imported items (e.g. nail wires and spare parts) because (1) the original producers of the items will obviously set prices that will cover the various costs associated with the production and delivery of the items plus some reasonable profit margins, before their Ghanaian distributors or agents assume ownership of them. (2) The distributors or importers of the production inputs will also have to set reasonable prices to cover their various costs (e.g. import duties, storage, and delivery) plus satisfying profit margins. Before the nail producers get the production inputs, the prices would be well over the factory prices. Even where the nail producers import the production materials by themselves, they will have to pay import duties plus the

> costs of the materials. The imported production inputs, in combination with other materials, will be used in producing nails for the local market. Consequently, raw material costs, production costs, overhead costs, packaging costs (purchase of local cartons), and marketing costs (e.g. sales tax), will have to be taken into consideration when setting prices on the finished nails in Ghana.

Faced with the above cost structures and/or market conditions, the Ghanaian nail producing companies all seem to set similar prices on their nails, taking their costs and the competitor prices into consideration. According to the managing director of Shasha, it was almost a norm in the market regarding the setting of prices on nails. For instance, he contended, a 2.5 kilogram of nails was sold for old Ghanaian 110 cedis by Shasha. And everywhere in the nail market, a 2.5 kilogram of nails, at the old Ghanaian110 cedis, was what all nail producers sold their nails for; there was virtually price transparency in the market. At this price of old Ghanaian 110 cedis per 2.5 kilogram, all the local competitors seemed to have satisfying returns.

But, since 2005, the local nail market has been 'invaded' by the Chinese and Indian nails which are imported into Ghana. The imported nails from China or India are finished products, already packaged and shipped to Ghana. Whether the tax structure for such imported goods is effective or not, the managing director suspects that the foreign nails are being dumped into the Ghanaian market because the managing director sees no reason why the sales agents of the Chinese and/or Indian nails can under price their nails, in comparison with what the local competitors charge for their nails. For example, 2.5 kilograms of Chinese or Indian nails are sold for 105 or 108 old Gahaian cedis, well below the old Ghanaian 110 cedis which all local competitors charge for a similar quantity of nails. According to the managing director, the local producers of nails, due to their cost structures, cannot compete with the imported nails, which are suspected to be subject to lower import taxes. The effects of this development are reported as follows:

> Some Ghanaian nails producing companies have already closed down (e.g. Sahara, a big competitor).

> Many will have to follow soon, if the situation is not addressed. Shasha Company is now producing 10 tons of nails a month instead of the 20 tons a month it used to do in the past, 50 % below capacity. Its number of permanent employees has now been reduced to four instead of the usual six; this time no part time workers are needed. The same can be said about the other Ghanaian nail producing companies; they are also facing reduced market shares and are producing far below capacity.

As said before, the managing director of Shasha is considering closing down his nail company next year, if the suspected 'dumping' strategies of the Chinese and Indian nail producers are not addressed in Ghana. When asked why Shasha Company and other nail producers in Ghana can't offer high quality nails and effective services to be highly competitive in the market, the managing director of Shasha had the following answer:

> "The strategy of the Chinese is to finance their Ghanaian agents to do personal selling, knocking at retailers' doors to offer cheap nails. Since most final users of nails have low purchasing power, they switch to buying of Chinese nails, which are relatively cheaper than the locally produced nails. In spite of the fact that the Chinese nails are of inferior quality compared with the locally produced nails, the lower price alone becomes a major competitive weapon for the Chinese. We cannot match them in terms of price, for our costs are very high. But the Chinese are dumping their goods here just to wipe away the local nail manufacturing capacity, which generates more employment. By just exporting finished products into Ghana, the Chinese are building their nail manufacturing capacity in China at our cost. I would prefer that instead of exporting finished nails to Ghana that they must come to produce nails in Ghana."

Let us now dwell on some discussions regarding the necessity to create an enabling environment for entrepreneurs, such as the managing director of the Shasha Company, to be able to meet competition, no matter where it comes from.

Discussion of the mini case

An enabling environment would consist of: availability of reliable industrial infrastructure, high proportion of local content instead of high proportion of imported goods/service in business activities in all sectors, efficient and regular supply of electricity and water, low inflation rate, a strong local currency, and easy access to affordable bank loans. The opposite developments of these features would be a lack of enabling environment in Ghana as has been pointed out elsewhere (Awuah, 1994; Asante et al, 2000; Kuada and Sorensen, 2001; FIAS, 2003).

Yielding to Caves' advice (1982), a country like Ghana would need to encourage and support entrepreneurs within the country that would help fill the country's cells in the input-output table, which is very empty. The linkages from the input-output relationships would, among other things, reduce many sectors' reliance on foreign inputs, which are also a major drain on the country's balance of trade or balance of payment. For years Ghana has suffered a negative balance of payments because many sectors, manufacturing, agriculture, health and education (Roe, 1991; World Development Report, 1990, 1994) rely heavily on foreign production inputs. The nail market discussed above is a case in point in modern times.

Subscribing to Caves (1982, pp. 270-271), the nail companies create backward linkages as they purchase their production inputs from other firms or suppliers. They create forward linkages by supplying their outputs, which become inputs to other processes and activities. In concrete terms, the nail producers' backward linkages bring about businesses to suppliers of nail wires, cartons, lubricants, petroleum, and services such as transportation of production inputs. The forward linkages which they generate have to do with final users of nails buying nails from retailers. The retailers buy their nails from distributors, who in turn, buy nails from the producers of nails. Each and every one of the inter-connected actors involved in the nail business has one or more employees, permanent or part-time. Shasha alone, a relatively small nail company, had been employing six permanent and some part-time workers in good times. Since the approximately 20 Ghanaian nail producing companies generate employment for people in Ghana, the employees certainly spend their earned incomes on some goods and services produced in the country. The end effect of the linkages is a major contribution to economic growth.

The absence of local production inputs, as the nail producers' situation portrays, will discourage entrepreneurs to emerge and exploit whatever market opportunities they have envisioned. Similarly, the absence of markets for locally produced goods and services in Ghana, where local producers are ill-prepared to face intense competition from foreign finished goods, will also discourage entrepreneurs to take the risk in investing. This is a situation which needs to be avoided if Ghana is to be able to generate a sustainable economic growth in the face of the impact of globalization and liberalization (see the next chapter).

Summary

In summary, this chapter has dwelled on the need for Ghana to encourage and support the creation of an entrepreneurial base, which would help bring about a sustainable economic growth. In this regard, the creation and the sustenance of an enabling environment, as the discussion of the situation of the nail producers in Ghana in this section has shown, is important for the development of firms. Once Ghana subscribes to the principles of market economy because the country cannot afford to isolate itself from the global community, efforts must be made to create the enabling environment, which will permit entrepreneurs to emerge and grow. The entrepreneurs must be able to compete with any competitor that enters the Ghanaian market, be it a Chinese, Indian, German or Brazilian firm. In Ghana it appears that the few entrepreneurs or firms that do risk investing in the country soon fade out when foreign competitors enter the Ghanaian market (Roe, 1991; Asante et al., 2000; Panford, 1994; Awuah, 1997).

The 1980s and most of the 1990s witnessed a mass closure of Ghanaian firms as the market was liberalized and foreign goods were imported into the country. Notably, textile, pharmaceutical, and food processing Ghanaian industries have all closed down due to increased competition from imports of finished goods that cater to similar needs, which the

Ghanaian firms sought to satisfy. And now we see that the nail industry is the next in line to be kicked away by imports of finished nails.

Apparently, the Ghanaian firms may not expect the government to be able to provide an enabling environment, when entrepreneurs do not complement that effort by demonstrating their ability to innovate in new products, new ways of marketing their goods/services, and new ways to interact with their target customers. Innovative solutions that are perceived by customers to be new and superior to alternative ones (Doyle and Stern, 2006) from competitors (no matter where they come from) will be preferred by customers. But, innovative solutions can, most of the time, be beyond the provision of a single firm. Hence, referring back to our model in Chapter One (Figure 1), the interaction between the government, businesses and the public will help create a forum where ideas, expertise, knowledge, and experiences can be shared. It is all about how to build a sustainable entpreneurial base, which will serve as one of the essential engines of fuelling economic growth that will benefit all in the society. To this end, the Ghana government should encourage and support collaboration between universities, other areas of higher learning and industries. Ghana should use sound fiscal and monetary policies to help and protect local industries. And firms must begin to learn how to compete and to co-operate with each other (even with competitors) at the same time. The challenges of globalization and liberalization of trade demand such a change in business orientations. In the next chapter we will discuss the impact of globalization and liberalization of trade.

References

Andersson, S. (2000). Internationalization of the Firm from an Entrepreneurial Perspective, *International Studies of Management & Organization*, Vol. 30 No. 1, pp. 63-92.

Asante, Y., Gyasi, E.M., and Tsikata, G.K, (2000). *Determinants of Foreign Direct Investment in Ghana*, Overseas Development Institute, Portland House, Stage Place, London SW1E 5DP.

Awuah, G. B. (1997). Promoting Infant Industries in Less Developed Countries (LDCs): A Network Approach to Analyze the Impact of the Exchange Relationships between

Multinational Companies and Their Indigenous Suppliers in LDCs' Efforts to Boost Infant Industries' Development; *International Business Review*, 6 (1), 71-87.

Awuah, G.B., (1994). *The Presence of Multinational Companies (MNCs) in Ghana: A Study of the Impact of the Interaction between an MNC and Three Indigenous Companies*, Dissertation, Uppsala University, Uppsala.

Caves, R.E., (1982). *Multinational Enterprise and Economic Analysis*, Cambridge Press University.

Deakins, D. (1999). *Entrepreneurship and Small Firms*. Cambridge. The University Press.

Delmar, F. (1996). *Entrepreneurial Behaviour and Business Performance*. Stockholm. Stockholm School of Economics.

Development Debate (2007). Debate on some development paths taken in Ghana, available at: http://www.ghanaweb.com/GhanaHomePage/NewsArchives/artikel.php?ID=119493: (Accessed, February 2, 2007)

Doyle, P, and Stern, P. (2006). *Marketing Management and Strategy* (4ed.). England, Prentice Hall.

FIAS (2003), *Ghana: Administrative Barriers to Investment Update*, Accra.

Kuada, J and Sorensen, O.J., (2001). Firms in the South: Interactions between National Business Systems and the Global Economy. In: Jakobsen, G and Torp, J.E (Editors), *Understanding Business Systems in Developing Countries*, Sage Publications, New Delhi/London.

Panford, K. (1994). Structural Adjustment, the State and Workers in Ghana: An African Development, *Quarterly Journal of the Council for the Development of Social Science Research*, Codesria, Dakar.

Porter, M. (1998). *Competitive Strategy: Techniques for Analyzing Industries and Competitors*, New York, The Free Press.

Roe, A.R. (1991). *Economy*. In Regional Survey of the World: Africa South of Sahara (1992), (21st Ed.). London, Europe Publications Limited.

Schlosser, E. (2002). *Fast Food Nation: What the All American Is Doing to the World*. London. Penguin Books Ltd.

Schumpeter, J.A. (1934). The Theory of Economic Development. Cambridge, MA. Harvard University Press.

Storey, D.J. (1998). *Understanding the Small Business Sector*. London, International Thomson Business Press.

World Development Report, (1994). *Infrastructure for Development*. Published for the World Bank, Oxford University Press, Oxford/New York/Toronto.

Chapter Seven

The Impact Of Globalization And Liberalization Of Trade

The world has now become a global village, an expression that is on almost everyone's lip these days. In the twinkling of an eye, those that are equipped with modern information technological devices (e.g. Internet, electronic mails, satellite and cable television sets, cell phones, and fax machines) will be informed of news and/or events that make headlines anywhere in the world. With the help of modern technology, these integrated means of connecting people across the globe are witnessed in many areas of human activities, not just the area of information sharing among people. As one author asserts (Lee, 2005), the world's move towards global integration produces the effect that the entire world's productivity has grown rapidly. Our tastes, needs, wants and demands are converging, a trend that has earned the description "Global Consumers" (Lee, 2005). Technology, for instance, is said to have made isolated places and impoverished people eager for modernity's allurements (Cox and Enis, 1988). Hence, almost everyone, everywhere, is said to want to have all the things they have heard about, seen, or experienced via the new technologies (Cox and Enis, 1988, p. 292). But, as expressed elsewhere (Human Development Report, 2002), the potential benefits which the new era of global integration offers will not be realized unless more of the world's people are included. Below we will look a little closer at some definitions of the term 'globalization', something which might facilitate one's analysis of the phenomenon and its implications.

Globalization

The term globalization, according to Curry (2000), refers to the worldwide phenomenon of technological, economic, political and cultural exchanges.

For Czinkota and Ronkainen (2007), the term globalization reflects a business orientation based on the belief that the world is becoming more homogeneous and that distinctions between national markets are not only fading but, for some products, will eventually disappear.

"Globalization is something of a cliché, but it is also a reality for governments. Even governments that have been relatively insulated from international pressures find that almost all their policies have an international dimension, and that those international pressures tend to force broader consideration of the issues" (Peters and Pierre, 2006, p. 122).

Although different emphasises can be deduced from each of the above illustrations of globalization, there are some common denominators to which all can be reduced. Apparently, there are global linkages, which make the interdependence among countries, governments, institutions, firms, and private individuals profound. Looking at the global linkage at the country or governmental level, the following three elements (Peters and Pierre, 2006) of globalization become worthy to discuss.

1. Global spread of ideas and practices
2. Market globalization
3. Ideas and market forces

Global spread of ideas and practices

A practice or a change that has spread rapidly across almost all countries concerns the need to undertake divestiture of public assets. On the one hand governments, as a way of copying ideas implemented elsewhere, may seek to consciously reap the financial benefits of enterprises and other asset sales (Peters and Pierre, 2006, p. 386). On the other hand, governments may be under pressure from the World Bank, International

Monetary Fund, and other international or regional lending agencies to divest their public assets. The global linkages at the governmental level, therefore, can have domestic policy repercussions (Czinkota and Ronkainen, 2007) in that both external and external forces can influence that.

Market globalization

As argued elsewhere (Peters and Pierre, 2006), governments are faced with the strong need to deal with international competition and investment. In that regard, governments are intent on divesting enterprises, notably in the airlines, banking and communication sectors, as a means of opening them up directly to international market forces and equity. The net result, as hoped, would be to expand their scope of influence, enhancing their performance, and increasing their financial resources.

Ideas and market forces

Governments are known to have considered certain assets to be of strategic significance. For example, utilities such as electricity, gas and water can be run by some private investors, albeit with some form of state regulation (Peters and Pierre, 2006, p. 387). In some cases, a government will partially divest some selected enterprises. This might result in mixed public and private ownership. Here, the impetus is the government's need to enjoy the best of both worlds. The rationale is that a government will be able to acquire needed resources from the sales involved, while still retaining a degree of internal control through the ongoing exercise of ownership rights.

Ghana's involvement in the globalization process

Relating Ghana's involvement to the above three elements of globalization, we find some actions of the government, which have been inspired by its own initiative to join the 'bandwagon' of the globalization (Peters and Pierre, 2006) process. Almost every nation seems to see some remedy in the dictates of globalization, to be integrated into the world trade and to reap the benefits associated with the integrated world markets. However, Ghana's involvement in the process of globalization is, in large, externally induced. The country has, since the 1980s until recent times (Tangari, 1991; Appia-Kubi, 2001), been under constant pressure from the World Bank, International Monetary Fund, and other international agencies to divest their public assets. The divestiture of poorly performing public enterprises might bring about better management, efficiency, and improved economic performance. As reported in Appia-Kubi (2001, p.39), Ghana's privatization programme generated about 14 % of the country's GDP between 1987 and 1999. The country could be seen to be on the right track, but that was not quite enough (p. 39). This external pressure has been very crucial in getting most countries to become involved in the globalization process. The International Monetary Fund (IMF) and the World Bank will demand that the country declare its willingness to be involved in the globalize world trade for credits or loans which a country might need from such bodies. The globalize world trade requires that countries reduce or eliminate their import and export duties, open their markets, privatize state enterprise and, above all, reduce or remove state subsidies (Spiegel Special, 2007: p. 114).

In Ghana's situation, the total submission to the dictates of globalization, the example being a high rate of divestiture of public enterprises, has not been possible to implement in Ghana. This is due to a number of reasons. It was reported in Tangari (1991) that the process of privatization in Ghana under the Provisional National Defence Council (PNDC) was very minimal. Other factors such as high outstanding credit sales, high costs of divestiture, and high outstanding liabilities of privatised firms have all contributed to the suboptimal results expected from the divestiture of public enterprises (Appia-Kubi, 2001). Political will to divest public enterprises is also said to be very low (Tangari, 1991; Appiah-Kubi, 2001). For Tangari (1991, p. 523), political impediments have been in the way of wholesale privatization. However, a number of other reforms such as trade liberalization, removal of most subsidies and incentive packages for potential investors have all been carried out with varied results (Roe, 1991; Panford, 1994; World Development Report, 1994; Asante et al., 2000; FIAS, 2003). All this suggests that joining the 'bandwagon' of globalization and doing as all other countries do or being forced to implement policies prescribed by foreign entities might not produce the same envisaged results obtained elsewhere. This is because what works well for one country may fail for another, depending on the capabilities, histories, resources and even the cultures of each. In this regard, trade liberalization, one important demand of globalization, needs be discussed.

Trade liberalization

Due to its strong appeal to enhance the increased productivity of our integrated markets, a number of transnational institutions such as the General Agreement on Tariffs and Trade (GATT), signed in 1947, The World Trade Organization (WTO), an institution that replaced GATT in 1995, IMF, the World Bank and Regional Institutions (EU, NAFTA, ECOWAS, and ASEAN) have emerged to encourage and support free trade among our integrated markets (Todaro, 1994; Czinkota and Ronkainen, 2007; Spiegel Special, 2007). For almost 60 years, beginning with the inception of the GATT, the world has expressed the urgent need to dismantle barriers of trade between countries; however, we still have partial submission to such a free trade, especially by the richer countries. The following quotation illustrates this point:

> "In principle, participating in the global market offers the same benefits as a flourishing market economy within a country. But, global trade is highly regulated, with the powerful holding sway and the playing field far from level. The average poor person in a developing country selling into global markets confronts barriers twice as high as the typical worker in industrial countries, where agricultural subsidies alone are about $1 billion a day – more than six times total aid. These barriers and subsidies cost developing countries more in lost export opportunities than the $56 billion in aid they receive each year.
>
> If there were levelling of the global playing field, many of the gains would come in low-income, low-skill areas such as agriculture, textiles and clothing. So in many cases both the poorest countries and the poorest people would benefit. Eliminating trade barriers and subsidies in industrial countries that inhibit imports from developing countries is therefore an urgent priority, and potentially a

> route to greatly accelerated development" (Human Development Report, 2002, pp. 31-33).

Ghana, for instance, has been accused of having over-liberalized its economy to the detriment of her people (Roe, 1991; Tangari, 1992; Panford, 1994). For example, many economic agents, such as manufacturing firms, have not had the ability to quickly re-orientate their strategies, technologies and their entire business conduct that would enable them to cope with new opportunities and new threats which have emerged from the increased competition as the result of trade liberalization. But, this incapability of local firms to face up to the forces of globalization and its concomitant demand of privatization, deregulation, and trade liberalizations is not the whole story. Still the global playing field for economic agents is not level, as one would expect. Hence the following question is legitimate. Where is the borderline for trade liberalization?

As reported elsewhere (Spiegel Special, 2007: p. 114), the European tax payers are said to have paid, just in 1997, 300 million Euros in export subsidies, which made it possible for the overproduction in their domestic market to be sent, at dumping prices, to the poorest countries of the world. When the U.S.A. refused in June 2006 to cut their agriculture subsidies, a group of developing countries, led by India and Brazil, acted to bring the collapse of the WTO's attempt to have trade negotiations among its member states (Spiegel Special, 2007: p.115). When the much needed trade negotiations among WTO member countries will come again is now uncertain. If the European Union and the U.S.A. continue to give subsidies to their farmers (Spiegel Special, 2007, pp. 114-115), do poor countries such as Ghana and other African countries have any chance to compete in the global markets? The mini case in Chapter Six, where Chinese firms are suspected to have dumped their finished nails in the Ghanaian market, is also a case in point, illustrating the chanceless situation facing most indigenous firms in Ghana.

Global linkages at the company and individual level

As the above discussions have shown, the linkages of states, seen from the governmental level, trickle down to companies and private individuals in any country that has joined the processes of globalization and its trade liberalization. Ghana, like many other countries, has opened its markets for all firms.

Linkage at the company level

The dismantle of trade barriers (e.g. removal of most physical, fiscal, monetary, and technical barriers) has made it possible for firms to enter and operate in almost any market of their choice, if their offers are competitive to enable them to win the choice of potential customers. For most companies survival is questionable if they are to solely concentrate only in their domestic markets. Presence in many markets of the world is a necessity for companies operating in global industries (Czinkota and Ronkainen, 2007) such as cars, banking, consumer electronics, entertainment, pharmaceuticals, publishing, travel services and home appliances. The need to be in global markets is illustrated in the following quotation:

> "Take, for example, pharmaceuticals. In the 1970s, developing a new drug cost about $ 16 million and took four years. The drug could be produced in Britain or United States and eventually exported. Now, developing a drug costs as much as $1 billion and takes as long as 12 years, with competitive efforts close behind. For the leading companies, annual R&D budgets can run to $ 5 billion. Only global products for global markets can support that much risk" (Czinkota and Ronkainen, 2007, p. 190).

The above quote is an example of one of the factors that can drive most global companies, operating in global industries, to take advantage of the opened markets, which now characterize our globalize world. Especially, most Japanese and American companies aggressively penetrate foreign markets by providing products which are good in quality and are competitively marketed (Cox and Enis, 1988; Czinkota and Ronkainen, 2007). The Chinese companies, according to Czinkota and Ronkainen (2007, p. 189), have entered the main markets of the world such as Europe and North America, with products ranging from auto parts and appliances to telecommunications, to become a global powerhouse.

For Czinkota and Ronkainen (p. 189), having a global presence ensures viability against other players in the home markets as well. All this suggests that companies in Ghana and any other country in the developing world, due to the forces of globalization and trade liberalization, cannot play it safe in their own domestic markets. The Chinese are also said to have been invading Africa with their products (Spiegel Special, 2007: p. 113 - 115). From Ghana's remotest corner to its major cities, there is an abundance of products coming from some world global companies. If Ghanaian companies do not go abroad to pre-empt or match competition there, their competitors will come and compete or pre-empt them in their own markets. In Ghana's case this has already happened, as some of the previous chapters have shown. As foreign companies, facing no trade restrictions whatsoever, come to offer good quality products at competitive prices to Ghanaian consumers, while their Ghanaian competitors (the indigenous ones) offer something inferior, ultimately the former will take over the market. Something needs to be done, then. Let us briefly look at the linkages at the individual level and their implications.

Global linkages at the private individual level

Due to the globalization and the trade liberalization forces that have swept across all countries, consumers everywhere on the global have a greater access to products and services, which the world has never known before (Czinkota and Ronkainen, 2007; Human Development Report, 2002). Products range from German cars, Japanese cameras and electronics, Brazilian coffee, American movies and music, Indian software, and textiles from China. As noted elsewhere, some of the new global players (e.g. "Mininationals" or "Born Globals") are able to serve the world from a handful of manufacturing bases (Czinkota and Ronkainen, 2007, p. 191; Doole & Lowe, 2004). Most firms are not required, in this era of globalization and trade liberalization, to build a plant in every country as some established multinational corporations once had to do. Now in the major cities in Ghana, there are an abundance of Internet Cafés, which are equipped with computers from companies located in the U.S.A. or Europe. Software to run the computers is produced in India or some other Asian or European countries.

The diffusion of mobile phones is overwhelming in Ghana today; modern vehicles, private and commercial ones, are also abundant in Ghana. The example of the mobile phone is worthy of illustrating.

> "Not long ago very few people had private telephones that worked. As recently as 1996, the telephone density of Ghana was 0.26% meaning that there were 2.6 telephone lines for every 1,000 people including 35 payphones in the entire country out of which 32 were located in Accra. This was one of the lowest in Africa. Today there is one phone for every four Ghanaians!
>
> This tremendous increase in the tele-density has been a result of the establishment of the National Communications Authority (NCA) in 1997 and the subsequent deregulation of the telecom industry, which brought about the growth of wireless telephony as a result of significant investment by operators. For the consumer, being in touch simply means being able to purchase a mobile handset and subscribing to a wireless service.
>
> Deregulation also meant opportunities for ambitious entrepreneurs and large telecom companies to establish operations in Ghana and participate in what was to become the biggest boom in Ghana's recent economic history" (Development Debate, 2007).

But, for all these products, the example being the mobile phones, the manufacturers can serve the Ghanaian market from abroad, without having to come to produce them in Ghana. These are goods that are well valued by customers and, hence, they want to have them. And with the intensified competition among the world marketers, the seller that produces 'value for the money' wins a customer's choice to do business with it (.i.e. the selling firm). Customers go for goods/services that are perceived to meet their 'total benefits' (Doyle and Stern, 2006). American, European and Asian goods/services are preferred by most customers in Ghana and in most developing countries because they are of good quality and are price competitive. Or the products/services from these areas might even be subsidized by their domestic tax payers to enable them to dump the goods/services cheaply in poorer countries (Spiegel Special, 2007). While the global linkages at the various levels present opportunities because governments, firms, and private individuals all, to a greater extent, have the chance to trade with whichever country, firm, and private individual they choose, thanks to globalization and liberalization of trade, there are enormous challenges which need to be overcome before the full-scale advantages of the globalization can have some recognizable impact on many poor people in the poorest countries of the world, as pointed out in the Human Development Report (2002, pp. 31-33).

Some suggestions to boost the competitiveness of Ghana

A government needs be pro-active to exploit the benefits of globalization

It is true that a government, in privatizing its public enterprises, relegates the competitiveness of the nation to how well private firms perform in the face of competition, especially from abroad, as the direct consequences of globalization. However, private firms will perform well, when there is an enabling environment in which to operate (see evidences provided in Chapter Six). In the globalized world, a country that is not pro-active to foresee the changes in technologies, demographics, living standards, political forces, lifestyles, fashion, and customer needs (Doyle and Stern 2006; Prahalad and Hamel, 1996) so as to provide a favourable condition for firms to be able to cater for the new needs that have emerged because of the changes, places the country in an uncompetitive position. The changes, some occurring gradually and others suddenly, bring about new needs. The Ghanaian market is full of advanced and/or new products/services that are more efficient than current ones.

Unfortunately, most of the new and efficient solutions to customers' needs come from overseas markets as finished goods to out-compete the locally produced alternative products/services. The indigenous firms' products/services are not preferred because they are perceived or even actually are experienced as being poorly designed, packaged, or of poor quality, and are even more expensive. But, whom does a customer prefer to do business with, in the midst of the abundance of goods/services that attracts a customer with a low purchasing power? One CEO of a multinational company in Ghana had the following to say about who gets the consumer's choice when it comes to purchasing a product/service.

> "We are operating in an economy where real income level is not rising at the same rate as the level of costs of goods. The majority of the people have already low income, so their purchasing power becomes greatly reduced. Paradoxically, consumers have greater variety of goods to choose from. The effect is that the most essential goods are bought first, a fact which is explained by the relatively low purchasing power currently in existence in the economy.
>
> Unless one is very efficient in satisfying the needs of the consumer, one is not likely to get larger share from the limited money of the consumer. The strategy by competing firms will be, among other things, (1) price reduction (i.e. price war) in order to win the consumer; (2) efficiency by way of controlling costs and working efficiently to produce better goods; and (3) efficiency of supplier in that efficient supplier will be able to reduce costs of goods supplied" (Awuah, 1994, p. 133).

The Ghanaian economy is still, a decade after the above facts were reported, plagued by the masses having very low purchasing power thus making it difficult for them to meet their basic needs in the midst of the abundance of goods/services in the Ghanaian market. Some pressure groups are even threatening the government to do something about the economic situation of the masses, especially for the large unemployment among the youth to be reduced drastically; else they will mobilize a mass demonstration against the government's neglect of the majority of the people (Development Debate, 2007).

Apparently, there are ample opportunities for the Ghanaian firms to produce goods/services for the majority of the Ghanaian people who go to the marketplace to look for means to satisfy their needs. But, many Ghanaian firms are not able to compete with the imported goods/services. This is because they face high costs structures and are not able to provide innovative and qualitative solutions to help meet customer needs better than foreign competitors are doing. However, some of the Ghanaian firms' problems are, quite often, blamed on the lack of the enabling environment. For instance, without a regular supply of electric power and running water, access to competitive bank credit, access to most critical production inputs in the domestic market, high overall cost levels, and proper policy framework to guide economic agents (see e.g. FIAS, 2003), Ghanaian firms will be at a disadvantage to compete with firms that come from an advanced environment to compete in Ghana.

The advances in science and technologies, as a means to foresee opportunities in the changes going on around us and how to exploit them, will require every nation to invest in the education of its labour force. Similarly, to foresee challenges/threats in the on-going changes will also require that the labour force in any country be educated and trained so as to be able to overcome any negative development, which the changes bring with them. In discussing the policy framework of Malaysia, for example, a reporter had this to say about the country: "Malaysia's socio-economic and political policies are congenial to the conduct of business in that country. The country is also said to have qualified personnel, favourable business climate and cost levels, and well-developed infrastructure, plus a strong support from the government for industries. All this has made Malaysia become very attractive as a place for foreign direct investment for many investors" (DI. Wednesday October 20, 2004: 17).

In view of the above, the Ghana government will have to be pro-active by having an enabling environment, manifested in investments in educating the people along the current trends, ability to use modern science and technologies, and actively stimulate and support business firms. Again, here the interaction between the actors mentioned in our model in Chapter One will be of relevance. The government will have to budget funds to enable places of higher learning (universities and research institutes), financial institutions and industries to collaborate in bringing about innovative products/services and production processes, which would boost the development of the industrial capacity of the entire country. The opportunities and challenges emerging from the globalization and trade liberalization are well beyond the solution of a single country and a single company. Hence, a government would need to actively interact with some of the actors identified in our model (see Chapter One) so as to leverage their complementary activities and resources, which would enable them to meet the challenges posed by the increased competition on the global scale.

For firms, their internal skills, knowledge, and activities would have to be upgraded and continually developed to be well-suited to the new economic opportunities and challenges. Chapter Eight serves to illustrate how the La Palm Beach Hotel's re-orientation compares to world standards of using modern technology to interact with customers worldwide. By the use of the Internet, La Palm Beach Hotel is providing its potential and current customers, all over the world, a 24-hour access to instantaneous product/service information and the ability to make cross-border purchases from their homes. The same cannot be said about many other firms operating in diverse industries in Ghana.

For example, the fast food industry has been in existence in Ghana for a long time, yet the indigenous entrepreneurs operating in the industry are still using outmoded technologies or practices, with the result that they lose customers to a few companies that have entered the market and are providing customers with modern and sophisticated means of meeting customer needs for fast food. In our fast-paced mood of going about our duties in big cities these days, responding to customer needs with innovative solutions more quickly would be a major competitive advantage. Well-learned, extensively-travelled, and wealthy customers needing to satisfy their hunger with fast food, because of lack of time, would go to the few fast food providers in our major cities, to spend 'heavy money' there to enjoy their quick meals in clean, comfortable surroundings with the sophisticated service delivery of food.

While the old practices of providing fast food abound everywhere in the cities and villages, and are relatively simple and cheap, people who are prepared to pay for superior benefits (cleanliness, comfortability, and good services) will go to the few modern fast food restaurants in the major cities. The modern fast food restaurants in Ghana are very few; in each major city there will be only about two or three. Their customer base is huge. With the use of modern technologies, service delivery systems, and the change of customer needs in their preference for modernity, the few fast food firms that offer modern solutions to satisfy customer needs better than their competitors can do (Prahalad and Hamel, 1996), will dominate the market. If the numerous small fast food providers are to compete with the modern ones, they will have to do a number of improvements. Education and/or training of the personnel, investment in modern equipment and processes to deliver good quality services, and above all, change of attitude regarding delivery of services to customers will all be very essential. The government needs to encourage and support small entrepreneurs either by stimulating the interaction between these firms and the places of learning so they might learn from each other during such interaction, or by financing research activities involving some places of learning and small businesses. This creates the enabling environment.

As we learned elsewhere in this book, most American fast food chains were started by door-to-door salesmen, short-order cooks, orphans, and dropouts, eternal optimists looking for a piece of the next big thing. Since the start–up costs of a fast food restaurant were low and the profit margins promised to be high, a wide assortment of ambitious people were seen buying grills and putting up signs (Schlosser, 2002, p. 22). Another important lesson had to do with men such as Kroc (McDonald's dynamic leader) and Walt Disney, both dropouts from high school, but who grew their businesses beyond all expectations (Schlosser, 2002, p. 33).

The whole world is a witness to how the McDonald's fast food chain and Disney have expanded not only in the U.S.A. where they originated, but throughout the world. Much of their expansive ability can be traced back to having started in an enabling environment. These 'dropouts' had the entrepreneurial ability to bring about businesses, which, in the course of time, could tap on the existing competencies in the environment, especially gaining access to well-educated and trained people who could help them access modern technologies and use them. A trend that needs be recommended for most Ghanaian firms is the ability to engage in collaborative arrangements with other firms, whose resources and activities complement theirs (Prahalad and Hamel, 1996; Ito and Rose, 2004). Collaborative arrangements between firms, a topic we shall return to in Chapter Nine, will enable firms to meet the challenges inherent in the multitude of demands which are put on firms; no single firm is capable of meeting such demands (Ito and Rose, 2004). Through collaborative arrangements, firms are able to combine their resources which enable them to meet the challenges of globalization.

Summary

In summary, all nations and any firm, anywhere, should bear in mind that no one is exempted from the impacts of globalization, negative or positive. A nation or a firm will need to have the foresight to know what the future, five, 10, and 15 years in advance, will mean in serving the multitude needs of customers. One will not only need to foresee changes well in advance of time, but must also have the capabilities to tap the opportunities inherent in those changes. Similarly, one will need to have the needed skills and knowledge to handle threats resulting from the changes. All in all, the forces of globalization and trade liberalization have come to stay for every nation and for every firm, so firms and governments need to re-orient themselves to be well-suited in addressing the challenges which the forces of globalization and trade liberalization bring to them. A country like Ghana can even go beyond its national boundaries and forge economic co-operations with countries within its immediate geographic region. For example, Ghana will need to intensify co-operations with countries in the Economic Region of West Africa, which have not been done until now. A glaring example is the recognition by the Scandinavian countries of the need to intensify regional co-oporation among their countries. In June 2007, the Nordic Prime Ministers came together to decide on common Nordic investments (GP: Sunday, 28 October, 2007: 63). This is something for Ghana and its regional neighbours. It would be imperative in the globalize world for firms to collaborate with other firms whose resources and activities are complementary to one's own (see Chapter Nine).

References

Appai-Kubi, K. (2001). State-Owned Enterprises and Privatization in Ghana, *The Journal of Modern African Studies* 39, pp. 197-229.

Asante, Y., Gyasi, E.M., and Tsikata, G.K, (2000). *Determinants of Foreign Direct Investment in Ghana*, Overseas Development Institute, Portland House, Stage Place, London SW1E 5DP.

Awuah, G.B., (1994). *The Presence of Multinational Companies (MNCs) in Ghana: A Study of the Impact of the Interaction between an MNC and Three Indigenous Companies*, Dissertation, Uppsala University, Uppsala.

Curry, J.E. (2000). *Internationales Marketing. Neue Märkte erschließen*, (Expansion im Zeichen der Globalisierung), Aus der Englischen Übersetzung. Von Jürgen Ulrich Lorenz, erste Auflage, Köln, Dt. Wirtschaftdienst.

Cox, K.K. and Enis, B.M (eds.). (1988). *Marketing Classics, a Selection of Influential Articles* (6th Ed.). London. Allyn and Bacon, Inc.

Czinkota, M.R., and Ronkainen, I. A. (2007). *International Marketing* (8th Ed.), United States of America. Thomson South-Western.

Dagens Industri. (Wednesday, October 20, 2004:17)

Development Debate (2007), Debate on some development paths taken in Ghana, available at: http://www.ghanaweb.com/GhanaHomePage/NewsArchive/artikel.php?ID=133752: (Accessed November 9, 2007).

Doole, I & Lowe, R. (2004). *International Marketing Strategy: Analysis, Development and Implementation* (4th ed.). London. Thomson Learning.

FIAS (2003), *Ghana: Administrative Barriers to Investment Update*, Accra.

Göteborgs Posten. (2007: Sunday, 28 October, 2007: 63)

Hamel, G. and Prahalad, C.K. (1996). *Competing for the Future*. Boston: Harvard Business School Press.

Human Development Report. (2002). Deepening Democracy in a Fragmented World, New York. Oxford University Press

Ito. K. and Rose, E.L. (2004). An Emerging Structure of Corporations. *The Multinational Business Review*. Vol. 12 No. 3. (Winter 2004). pp. 63-83

Lee, K. (2005). *Global Marketing Management: Changes, Challenges, and New Strategies*, England. Oxford University Press.

Panford, K. (1994). Structural Adjustment, the State and Workers in Ghana: An African Development, *Quarterly Journal of the Council for the Development of Social Science Research*, Codesria, Dakar.

Peters, B. G. & Pierre, J (2006). *Handbook of Public Policy*. London. Sage Publications.

Roe, A.R. (1991). *Economy*. In Regional Survey of the World: Africa South of Sahara (1992), (21st Ed.). London, Europe Publications Limited.

Schlosser, E. (2002). *Fast Food Nation: What the All American is Doing to the World*. London. Penguin Books Ltd.

Spiegel Special: Geschichte- Afrika, das umkämpfte Paradies, Nr. 2/22 – 05- 2007.

Tangari, R. (1991). The Politics of Divestiture in Ghana, *African Affairs*, Vol. 90. No. 361 (October), pp. 523-536.

Todaro, M.P., (1994). *Economic Development*, 5th edition, Longman Publishing, New York.

World Development Report, (1994). *Infrastructure for Development*. Published for the World Bank, Oxford University Press, Oxford/New York/Toronto.

Chapter Eight

The Use Of The Internet As A Marketing Strategy In The Hotel Industry: A Comparison Between Brazil, Ghana, And Sweden

A paper presented by Prof. Venilton Reinert (Universidade Regional de Blumenau, Brazil) and Assoc. Prof. Gabriel Baffour Awuah (Halmstad University, Sweden) at a conference in Joâo Pessoa, Brazil, in June 2007.

Abstract

The new information technologies (NIT), especially the Internet, have created opportunities for companies. NIT can be used as a tool to execute marketing activities on three levels: (1) a firm can convey information about its products and services, using various communications tools, (2) conduct transactions by means of e-commerce and deliver its products/services online or (3) by the help of the conventional delivering way. In the tourism market, which is an *information-oriented phenomenon,* the NIT has had strong influence because people use the Internet to search for information to better plan their trips. In the hotel business, for example, the customers search for the company's core service and support services, which can fulfill their basic and secondary needs. In this perspective, this study analyzed how hotels presented their services, prices, and communicated with their customers on the Internet. The main objective was to analyze the presentation of the marketing mix strategies in the hotels' websites. The methodology used was first an exploratory research and then a descriptive study. The method was a qualitative and the population was hotels from three countries, Ghana, Sweden and Brazil. The results showed that the information aired in the hotels' web pages were clearly directed to their respective target audience. To promote their services, the companies studied used, as their main communication tools, advertising, Customer Relationship Management (CRM) and public relations. It can be inferred that the companies uniformly used marketing and communication tools in their websites. Thus, to market their services, no difference was found among the three firms' use of those tools.

Keywords: Marketing mix, Internet, Strategy, hotels, Brazil, Ghana, and Sweden

Introduction

Searching for human and social development, the leaders of different societies, some pressured by its members, make investments in certain areas that promote the well-being of the individuals and community. The resources, depending on a group's priority, are targeted to strategic areas, such as health, education, technology, and general infrastructure. The results of these investments, when well applied, can be noticed in the growth of education level of the individuals and in the use of technologies, such as the Internet, as well as in the amount of money directed to leisure and entertainment.

When leisure comes into account, tourist activities have gained importance in the last few years. According to the World Tourism Association (2007), in the year 2006, the demand for tourism increased by 4, 5% compared to the previous year, which positions this activity among the ones with the higher growth rates on the planet. The directors of the World Trade Organization (WTO) mention that the increased rate was bigger than was expected and that the tourism sector has been facing a long period of sustainable economic expansion, which puts it among the most dynamic industries in an economy. International tourism represents more than one third of the business services around the globe; and it will continue to generate high economic growth in the next decade. As Ortega and Goncalez (2007) state, the tourism industry has turned out to be an important industry. It has contributed to make local, as well as national, economies stronger.

Kim, Letho and Morrison (2007) highlight that, due to its nature, tourism is an *information-oriented phenomenon* because of structural reasons. For Kim, et al (2007), the revolutionary development of the information technology has drastically changed the society and the lives of people, including the way in which the tourists search for information and plan their trips. According to Giovannini (2001), the new information technology (NIT), especially the Internet, has created great opportunities for firms. As advantages, Giovannini mentions the cost reduction in the buying process; selling and administrative services; the improvement of the supplies administration and the management of supplies; market and demand enlargement; growth of the offered values to the clients and communication improvement (making clients aware of products, solving their problems, identification of their necessities, and an attempt to get client's loyalty).

Whenever the offering of information by the companies to the clients is considered, Fodness and Murray (cited by KIM, LEHTO and MORRISON, 2007) define the search for information as a dynamic process, in which the individuals make use of different sources and different information with the main objective to facilitate the trip planning. They highlight that this information can be collected through sources which they call *marketing-dominated and non-marketing-dominated.* The *marketing-dominated* information comes from sources such as advertising in the mass media, brochures, tourist guides, portals and more recently the Internet. However, the *non-marketing-dominated information* can be encountered by the daily contacts with friends and family and through personal experiences.

It is important to mention that the Internet has become more and more a part of lives of the individuals and companies. For individuals, it can be used as entertainment, as well as a tool to communicate, and as an information supplier during the products and services purchase process. For companies, as a source of information, it is crucial to the development of marketing activities. As a communication tool, the firms make use of it as a means to integrate the various departments, as a way to maintain a good relationship with customers, as a medium to convey information about the firm's products and services, and as a way to sell goods and services. In this way, taking into account the multiple possibilities of Internet use and the strategic use of it as a means to achieve the marketing objectives, it plays an important role in the marketing field day by day.

Wright, Kroll, Parnel (2000) state that new technologies are affecting the companies' operation as well as their products and services:

> The recently achievement in computers, robotics, laser, satellite net, optics fiber and other related areas offered important opportunities to improve the company's operation. Industries, banks and retailers, for example, make use of this computer technologies advance to develop their traditional activities with low cost and with a high consumer satisfaction. The technology changes can exterminate existing companies' even entire sectors of economy, once the demand change from one product to another. (ID.,IBID., p.54).

In the organizational context, based on the agility of information technology and communication, Varadarajan and Yadav (2002) mention that the electronic marketing has started to gain emphasis. The above authors attribute the rise of electronic marketing to the following factors: a) richer information in the transactional environment; b) easier search for the information due to the quantity of information available; c) Smaller information power gap between seller and buyer; d) Less time passed between purchase and physical product bought in the electronic market.

Stalk (cited by Montgomery and Porter, 1998), referring to the velocity of happenings in the market, adverts that the time is one key advantage and that the way the leading firms manage their time in production, new product and services development, and selling and distribution, represent the most powerful competitive advantage.

To achieve competitive advantage in the actual market scenario is the main objective of the companies that, for this purpose, are utilizing more and more Internet marketing strategies. Huizingh (2003) highlights four strategic uses of the Internet: to add interaction to the product and services, to offer values to the actual consumers, to attract new consumers, and to restructure the distribution channel.

Related to the use of Internet by marketing managers, Bandvopadhyav (2001) states that it can be used to execute marketing activities in three levels: to provide information related to the company and its products through communication tools such as advertising, public relation, sales promotion and CRM (Customer relationship management), to conduct transactions and to allow consumers to reserve products and services which can be delivered by traditional mail or special services, as well as conduct transactions that can provide the physically delivered item.

Soumitra and Segev (1999, p. 470) discuss electronic marketing and make an analysis of the transformation that the 4Ps (product, price, place and promotion) have faced after the adoption of the Internet by the firms. They add an additional C (consumer) to this schema, which now has been called 4Ps+C. They mention that even though interactivity in real time between company and the diverse publics exists, and there exists a global connection through the Internet, 'the transformation is poor'. They detected, in the turn of the 20th and for the 21st century, that the companies have a long way to go in order to be able to explore the transformation power of the Internet, "except the item related to the customer relationship" (p. 475).

Varadarajan and Yadav (2002) explain that, in the competitive aspect, the strategy has the imperative function to explore the available resources to reach and maintain a competitive defense and the advantage position in the market. This way, a marketing strategy has its focus on the way the company must allocate its marketing resources to achieve and maintain the market competitive advantage.

In view of the above, the main objective of this study is to analyze the marketing tools (4Ps) which the studied hotel firms utilize in the presentation and sale of their respective services on the Internet. The specific objectives are to: identify the services offered, identify the availability of prices in the studied firms' respective websites, and analyze the communication tools adopted by the hotels (CRM – Customer Relationship Management, advertising, sales promotion, Public Relations, publicity and direct marketing) in their websites. We therefore seek to address the following research question: How does a firm present its products/services, price, and communicate with (e.g. using the CRM approach) its target customers on the Internet?

The rest of the paper will proceed as follows: The next section is devoted to the discussion of the theoretical framework, followed by the methodology used. Thereafter, the cases are presented, followed by the analysis. Finally, we present the conclusion of the study.

Theoretical framework

The approaches taken by the researches, related to the strategic marketing study, converge to the point that the observation of the market and its changes constitute a crucial element during the decision-making process, which leads a company to success. Thus, it can be assumed that the consumer's behavior changes, the competition, and the external factors (politics, legal, and climate), along with the technology innovation are factors to be considered in these constant changes in the market. Hence, to observe, to follow, and to decide, based on that information, are the main duties of marketing managers.

Whenever the consumer's behavior is considered, it is necessary to recognize that, according to Wind and Mahajan (2003), the Internet has changed the marketing priorities; it has given more power to clients. With technological tools available, consumers start to do their own research, creating communities and demanding exchanges in price, the way companies treat their clients, and other companies' strategies.

Sodre (2007), referring to the tourism market, mentions that there is an imperfect competition among companies such as hotel and travel agencies. He explains that two hotels do not offer the same services and comfortableness; and neither do two travel agencies offer the same travel packages and accommodations.

A model of services concept

In view of the above context, it can be affirmed that companies are in the market to meet consumers' needs. The need satisfaction level that the companies can generate will define the actual and future sales of their products and services (Doyle and Stern, 2006). In the tourism segment, especially in the hotel business, companies that try to reach a high level of consumer needs satisfaction must offer, besides the core services, other extra services (by-services and support services), as shown in the Figure 8.1 below, which exceed the client's expectation.

A. Customer Needs		**B. Design of Benefits (offers)**
Primary need	↔	Core service
Secondary need	↔	By-services and support services

Figure 8.1: The Model of Services Concept

Source: Edvardsson & Larsson (2004, p. 43).

Edvardsson and Larsson (2004) state that, in order to satisfy a client's needs, a service company must maintain a main service or a core service, to satisfy the consumer's basic needs, which are the primary needs of the consumer. Based on this core service, the company must make available other services, namely, by-services and support services, which will satisfy the secondary needs of the customer. For a hotel firm, a by-service (Grönroos, 1994; Edvardsson and Larsson, 2004) is the service which makes it possible to fully satisfy the primary needs of the customer. For instance, for a hotel client whose primary need is for accommodation, the core services offered by the hotel would be a furnished room, with all the necessary facilities to enable the client to sleep there. The by-services may include a 24-hour access to the reception. This is important because someone must be available to help the customer with additional services (tangible or intangible), if need be. Having bilingual and/or multilingual languages, especially when dealing with foreigners and even analphabets, would be an important by-service. The support services may include physical products such as a swimming pool, bar, restaurant, shuttle 24 hours, front desk, and others. Ability to satisfy both the primary needs and the secondary needs of a company's client is crucial for obtaining a competitive advantage in the marketplace.

Any attempt to satisfy both the primary and the secondary needs would be a way of offering the client 'total benefits', which almost all clients who choose to buy services are looking for. And this makes the provision of both by-services and support services, as complements to the core services, very important. The core services, complemented by the added values derived from both the by- and support services, might differentiate a firm's offers from those of its rivals. As Sodre (2007) maintains, there is no way two hotels can be seen offering the same and identical services or comfortableness. Using the Internet as a major medium of marketing to persuade clients to opt for one's offerings, the ability for a hotel firm to aid a client's search and choice of some core services and by- and support services which will satisfy the client's primary and secondary needs, is very crucial.

The above theoretical framework will aid our understanding of how the three hotels, in Brazil, Ghana, and Sweden, make use of the Internet to aid a client's search and choice of some core services as well as by- and support services. The framework also serves as our analytical tool.

Methodology

For the methodology, first an exploratory type of research to provide the researchers with information about the subject to be studied was developed. According to Malhotra (2001), the main objective of an exploratory research is to make it possible for the researchers to understand the problem being studied. This type of research tries to explore one problem or situation to create possibilities to determine criteria and understanding of it. To collect and analyze data, the qualitative method and a descriptive type of research were chosen. The qualitative method does not take into account a numeric representation, but it tries to aid a deep comprehension of a social group, an organization, and other elements. Minayo (1993) states that the qualitative approach incorporates the meaning and intention of the studied subject. However, the descriptive approach has the objective to know and get the interpretation of a reality without any interference and change (VIERA, 2002). In this type of investigation, the main interest is to find out phenomena, trying to describe, classify, and interpret them. According to Mattar (1996), the descriptive type of research is characterized by its well-defined objectives and its formal procedure; also, it is well-structured and directed to solve problems or to evaluate the different alternatives in action.

To define the population and sample of this study, Richardson's (1999) definition of population and sampling was used. For Richardson, one population or universe is the amount of elements that possess some determined characteristics and the sample is any part of the population or universe. Submitting to this view, it was defined that the population of this research would be Brazilian, Ghanaian and Swedish resort type hotels that offer a variety of services, besides the core services; and the hotels must be indigenous ones from the studied countries (i.e. they cannot belong to an international hotel chain).

Mattar (2000) highlights that, with a very good criteria and a proper strategy, the cases to be included in the research can be chosen. And in this way also, the samples that are satisfactory to the investigation can be decided. Mattar emphasizes that, in this type of sampling, the selection of the elements that constitute the population to be part of the sample depends, at least in part, on the judgment of the researcher or the field interviewer. There is no known chance that one element will be part of the sample. By this way, the sample used in this study consists of three hotels: Costão do Santinho Resort (Brazil), La Palm Royal Beach Hotel (Ghana), and Hotel Tylösand (Sweden). We present the cases below. All the information contained in the case section was obtained from the respective websites of the studied firms.

Presentation of the cases

Some basic information

The Costão do Santinho (Brazil) is located at Florinaopolis (SC). It is considered the best and the most luxurious tourist complex in southern Brazil. It has a complete infrastructure of services which are comparable to international patterns. It is considered to be one of the three best spa resorts in the country, with its facilities spread out over a 1 million square meter area. It has a leisure area, with an exuberant landscape, in a space of 750 thousand square meters of preserved Atlantic jungle.

The La Palm Royal Beach Hotel is located by the ocean in Accra, Ghana's capital. It is the first resort in the country; it was opened in 1999, and has a five-star classification. It is located a few minutes away from the city center, close to shopping malls and businesses. Its facilities are spread over a 300 thousand square meter area.

The Tylösand Hotel is located on one of the most popular beaches of Sweden, Tylösand, nine kilometers from the city center of Halmstad. Its facilities were first constructed in 1906, to be used as a bath house. The infrastructure was remodeled recently to give place to one of the most known four-star category hotel resorts in Sweden.

The information based on the websites of the companies, was collected and analyzed by two researchers fluent in the Ghanaian, English, Portuguese and Swedish languages. To orient the collection and analysis of the data, the following categories of information, price, service, and promotion, were developed as a guideline. The analysis started at the main home page of the studied companies. To verify the category of information analyzed, the researchers clicked on the correspondent link. Whenever the websites offered an option to read the information in English, the analysis was done in that language. However, after the English analysis, the researchers checked the information in the original language.

Services, price, and promotion as presented by the hotels

Place, an element of the marketing mix, is considered as the hotel itself. This is due to the nature of the services offered; for example, all the core services are provided in the hotels. The first specific objective refers to the presentation of the offered services by the hotel on their websites. In this research, the first attempt was to identify the core services, the by-services, and the support services offered by the companies. It was noticed that, according to the target audience, the information about the three types of services on the main web pages of the respective hotels was easy to notice; it was easy to see whom they were addressing.

The services

In the first web page studied, the Costão do Santinho (Brazil), the information on the main web page, was presented in text and photo formats, and targeted to families and tourists on vacation. The bed and breakfast and entertainment infrastructure, such as swimming pool, access to a green area, are the main services (core) offered by this hotel. Despite the unclear information on the main page, the spa services such as facial and body esthetic, relaxing massage, stone therapy and conference rooms also are part of the core services of this hotel.

It can be noticed that the Costão do Santinho Resort tries to serve three types of consumers. However, the main page contains information addressed to clients interested in leisure and relaxation with a larger emphasis on entertainment and accommodation. Whenever the secondary services are considered, Costão do Santinho Resort presents on its web page, a diversity of activities such as ecological trekking and wild beaches, multicultural parties, live shows, six restaurants, three bars, and other activities. For the by-services, all customer categories have access to the reception and through that may also receive help of any kind.

In the second web page studied, La Palm Royal Beach Hotel (Ghana), the information on the main page makes it clear that the main services (core services) are addressed mainly to business people and government delegations and secondly to tourists on vacation. The text information available mentions clearly that the offered infrastructure is for the first mentioned, while for the tourists they present the number of rooms available. Other activities, such as leisure and entertainment, which composed the core services, are presented through a diversity of links available on the main web page. Whenever the support services come into account, such as babysitters, airport shuttle, foreign currency exchange, rent-a-car and fitness center, they are communicated via the same link where the core services information is. For the by-services, all customer categories have access to the reception and through that may also receive additional help of any kind.

On the third website studied, Hotel Tylösand (Sweden), it could be noticed, through photos and texts, that the main attention (core services) targets two main groups: companies interested in using facilities to hold conferences and people searching for rest and relaxation. The information conveyed to the companies is available through a link that sends the customer to information about the facilities to hold a conference in the hotel, the number of rooms, and the size of a room. The information highlights 29 conference rooms and a congress hall, which are located in front of the sea, with capacity for 700 people. For the other target audience category, the website contains links with information about the offered services by the spa such as swimming pool for relaxation, physical activities such as spinning, yoga, stretch, and massage. As a secondary service, the company offers restaurants, piano bar, art gallery, horse riding, gastronomy experiences, fitness center, and other items that serve the two client categories. For the by-services, all customer categories have access to the reception, which can provide additional services, if need be. There is also information available about activities offered in the summer time (i.e. high season).

Prices

The second objective of this study refers to the verification of the availability of prices on the websites of the hotels. For the Costão do Santinho Resort, there is no information about the prices of its core service(s), bed and breakfast and spa; neither are there prices about the secondary services. The main page presents a link called "*pacotes e tarifas*". However, the client is required to fill out a form with personal information, including e-mail and telephone number, the period in which he/she wants to stay and the number of people that will come together. After this, the client receives an e-mail with the requested information. It is important to highlight that the information requested in the fill-out form is addressed to people living in Brazil. For example, the indication of the future client's home country is not asked.

On the La Palm Royal Beach Hotel's main website, the prices of accommodation are very clearly presented in the link *rates & reservations.* The prices are shown according to the type of room: *standard room single* $230, *standard room double* $250, *extra bed* $30, *junior suite single* $320, *double junior suite* $340, *presidential suite* $400 and *royal suite* $520. The price of the conference rooms and other special activities, defined by the hotel as "*special moments*", are not available. The prices of secondary services such as babysitter, beauty, saloon and secretaries, also are not presented at the web page.

On the Tylösand Hotel's website, one of the core services, the spa, the price is clearly shown in the correspondent link. The price of accommodation varies according to the type of package ordered by the client. The price can range from $200 a day, for the small spa & pleasure package, to $850 for the Tylösand de Luxe package. Related to the other core services, the conference rooms, the prices also are presented in packages that vary according to the group size and the time of the year that the conference will be held. For instance, for March, the price can range from $285 for one room for 20 to 40 people to $895 for a room with 240 places. However, for April, the price can differ from the ones charged on March. As with the other hotels researched, the price of the support services are not available.

Promotion

The third specific objective of this study refers to the communication tools used by the companies on their websites. On the first website studied, Costão do Santinho Resort, a strong use of advertisement can be noticed. This activity appears in the format of movement banners, bottoms, and rectangular figures. The banner is located on the top of the page with pictures of the leisure facilities. The bottom appears as a link to connect the consumer to diverse activities offered by the hotel. The rectangular figure is used in two sizes, one to take the consumer on a virtual tour of the hotel and the other to inform of the happenings in the hotel such as Easter parties and Davis Tennis Cup. Whenever the company's image comes into account, the hotel makes use of Public Relations, using three institutional bottoms and a one rectangular figure in movement. The first bottom is used as a (water stamp) over the main banner. It highlights the hotel's prize as the best resort hotel in Brazil in the years 2005 and 2006. The second one, in water stamp format, shows the hotel's logo and the third one connects to a link presenting information about the city of Florianopolis. The rectangular figure functions as a source of information about the happenings in the hotel. For CRM, the main marketing activity used by the hotel is a link such as "*relationship and talk to us*", in which the phone number is available for verbal contact.

In the study of La Palm Royal Beach Hotel, the data shows that the company uses advertising throughout four banners which contains text and photos; each one of them makes a link with the activities offered by the hotel, namely casino, golf field, Internet wireless, and restaurant. Other information, such as the number of rooms, the special swimming pool size, and entertainments, is presented in text format shown on the main web page. The sales promotion activity is also explored by the company throughout two banners, one static and the other in motion. Both of them make links with the offered services. The technique used for this activity is in the special discount format during the weekends and bonuses. For the client to know the amount of the discount or the bonus, he or she must click on the link to be able to retrieve this information. The institutional work (Public Relations) is showed with the use of the slogan "*uniquely golden, traditionally Ghanaian*" and with the use of the link called *"brochure"*. At this link the client can register him- or herself to receive news about the hotel, *newsletter*, *corporate information,* and an event schedule. Related to CRM, the link "contact us" is one of the direct channels between the client and the company.

For the Tylösand Hotel, it could be noticed that three different marketing and communication tools, advertising, public relations, and CRM are used. The advertising used/uses a moving banner to show the images of the conference rooms (one of the core services of this hotel), the company's product, a mineral water, the hotel's front desk and the art gallery. Besides the banner, the website shows the presence of two rectangular figures, with photos and text, which link with two services offered by the firm: the spa and the conference rooms. Whenever Public Relations come into account, two rectangular figures, also using photos and texts, link to the schedule of events in the hotels and the summer activities planned such as concerts, plays. The CRM tool is used only through the link "contact us".

Analysis

As was treated in the case section, the 'Place' (P) of the marketing mix, was considered as the hotel itself. For this reason, the analysis of this P is done together with the analysis of the services. With the 'P', the promotional element of the marketing mix, only communication tools present at the main websites of each hotel are analyzed.

To achieve a higher level of consumer needs satisfaction, especially with services firms, clearly offering core services, by-services and some support services (Grönroos, 1994; Edvardsson and Larsson, 2004) will boost a services firm's competitiveness. All three hotels in this study clearly provide various core services, by-services, and support services. For example, Hotel Costão do Santinho (Brazil) has bed and breakfast and entertainment infrastructure (e.g. swimming pool and access to green areas) as its core services, which are meant to meet the primary needs of customers looking for accommodation or looking for a place to entertain themselves. In addition, this hotel offers some by-services (e.g. access to the reception and bilingual languages) and some support services (e.g. ecological trekking, wild beaches, multicultural parties, live shows, restaurants, and bars).

The La Palm Royal Beach Hotel (Ghana) also provides the following as its main core services: bed and breakfast, leisure activities, facilities for conferences, and entertainment. Some of its by-services are a 24-hour access to the reception, where a client can get additional services besides the core services; also bilingual and/or multicultural languages are provided. The support services offered by this hotel are a babysitter service, airport shuttle, foreign currency exchange service, a car rental service, fitness centre, restaurants, and bars.

The core services of the Hotel Tylösand (Sweden) consist of facilities for conferences, bed and breakfast, and the spa services (e.g. facilities for rest and relaxation). Some of its by-services consist of customers' access to the reception, which will enable them get any other services besides the core ones. Its support services are restaurants, bars, and room services.

Since no two service firms provide exactly the same and identical services (Sodre, 2007), each of the three hotels in this study have different core services, which are directed to specific target groups whose primary and secondary needs are different. A close observation here will reveal that what seems to be a primary need of some target group(s) might be a secondary need of other target groups and vice versa. However, the provision of a 'total benefit' (Edvardsson and Larsson, 2004), which a customer seeks from a hotel firm has been found to consists of the offer of core services, by-services, and support services. Here, the by-services and the support services, which each of the three hotels offer, seems to be almost the same, at least from their description and/or purposes. All provide access to a reception (e.g. of a by-service) and all have support services such as restaurants, bars, and room services.

Varadarajan and Yadav (2002) mention that the electronic marketing facilitates the availability of richer information in the transactional environment. To make it possible, the companies have different marketing and communication tools available, to convey messages and also to work, in the relationship, with customers. In this study, it was noticed that the use of four different marketing and communication activities: advertising, public relation, sale promotion and CRM are common when one visits the websites of the studied companies.

In advertising, the firms made/make use of banners, with and without movement, bottoms and rectangular figures. The conveyed messages are directly related to the two types of services: the core and the secondary services. The sales promotion was used by only one company, La Palm Royal Beach Hotel. The technique used by the firm was a bonus to be used at the casino and special discounts to be used by the customers during the weekends. Related to public relations, this study detected that all the companies are preoccupied with their own respective images because all of them made/make use of this communication activity. The main tool used was/is a newsletter, which gives information about the happenings in the hotels. To develop a good relationship with customers (i.e. the use of CRM), the three companies make the link "talk to us" available; and some of the hotels, for a quick contact, have available a phone number.

As Varadarajan and Yadav (2002) maintain, the electronic marketing facilitates the availability of richer information in the transactional environment. This will have to make use of the Internet as a medium through which customers can be aided in their search and choice of some core services as well as by- and support services. Important information in this context, therefore, will be the price of any of the services provided. Related to price, it was verified that the ones related to the core service are clearly presented by two hotels, La Palm Royal Beach and Hotel Tylösand. The Costão do Santinho Resort does not make prices of its services available on the Internet. Since the hotels have different core services and some even do not state the prices of their core services, it is not possible to compare their prices with each other. In the next section we present a brief conclusion of this study.

Conclusion

The main objective of this study has been to analyze the marketing tools (4Ps), which a firm may utilize in the presentation and sale of its services on the Internet, an important electronic technology. The specific objectives are: to identify the services offered, to identify the availability of prices of the various services offered by a firm in its websites, and finally to analyze the communication tools adopted by the hotels. These are activities which are very essential to help customers search and choose a firm that offers a potential or a current customer clues as to what he or she is about to buy or is buying.

The marketing theory has a basic premise with regards to the need to satisfy the wants and desires of customers. Edvardsson and Larsson (2004), writing about services companies state that to satisfy the needs of a firm's clients, the companies must offer services that fulfill basic and secondary needs. For the above authors, the basic needs are the ones that the client tries to satisfy in the first place. In the hotel business, the bed and breakfast, for example, could be the first service that the client seeks to satisfy. Therefore, this type of service is named by Edvardsson and Larsson (2004) as the core service or the main service of the organization. The secondary needs are fulfilled by by-services and support services or complementary services. As far as the three hotels in this study are concerned, core services do differ, depending on the target group(s) being served. On the websites of the studied companies, it is possible to notice that all of them offer more than one core service. In the Costão do Santinho Resort, three core services are offered: the Bed and Breakfast and leisure, the spa, and the conference rooms. However, it is important to highlight that only one of the core services is emphasized on the main web page of this hotel. La Palm Royal Beach Hotel, offers two different types of core services: Bed and Breakfast and leisure, and the conference rooms facilities; both of them are highlighted on the main web page of the hotel. The Tylösand Hotel offers two core services: the infrastructure to hold conferences and the spa services, both of them are highlighted on the main page.

As far as the secondary services are concerned, it could be noticed that there are no main differences among the three hotels. All of them have restaurants, bars, room services, and other activities (e.g. transportation, and foreign exchange service), these being examples of support services. The by-services are, for example, a 24-hour access to the reception for any additional services which a customer may need while consuming the main core service(s). Thus, all the three firms see the need to offer by-services and support services as an essential compliment to the core services, which customers buy.

Regarding price information, only two of the three hotels, La Palm Royal Beach Hotel and Hotel Tylösand, have clear information for the core services offered. The Costão do Santinho Resort does not make prices of its services available on the Internet.

Submitting to Varadarajan and Yadav (2002), a firm's interaction with customers, through electronic medium, should facilitate the availability of richer information in the transactional environment. To make it possible, the companies have different marketing and communication tools available, which convey messages and also to work, in the relationship, with customers. In this study, it was noticed that the use of four different marketing and communication activities: advertising, public relation, sale promotion and CRM are common, when one visits the websites of the studied companies.

In advertising, the firms made/make use of banners, with and without movement, bottoms and rectangular figures. The conveyed messages are directly related to the two types of services: the core and the secondary services. The sales promotion was used by only one company, La Palm Royal Beach Hotel. The technique used by the firm was a bonus to be used at the casino and special discounts to be used by the customers during the weekends. Related to public relation, this study detected that all the companies are preoccupied with their own respective images because all of them made/make use of this communication activity. The main tool used was/is a newsletter, which gives information about the happenings in the hotels. To develop a good relationship with customers (i.e. the use of CRM), the three companies make the link "talk to us" available; and some of the hotels, for a quick contact, have available a phone number. Following Varadajaran and Yadav (2002) and Edvardsson and Larsson (2004), it could be inferred, based on the analyzed information, that the companies make a uniform use of the marketing and communication tools to present their core and secondary services. In other words, there are no significant differences between the marketing and the communication tools, which the firms use to present their core and secondary services in the Internet.

References

BANDVOPADHYAV, Moumaya. Competitive strategies for internet marketers in emerging markets. **Competitiveness Review**, v. 11, issue 2, p. 16, 2001.

DOYLE, PETER, AND STERN, PHILLIP, **Marketing Management and Strategy** (4th ed.), 2006, Edinburgh Gate: Pearson Education Limited.

EDVARSON, BO; LARSSON Patrik. **Tjänstegarantier**. kopieringsförbud, 2004. Sweden.

GIOVANNINI, Fabrizio. A empresa média industrial e a Internet. **Caderno de Pesquisas em Administração**, São Paulo, v. 8, n. 3, jul./set. 2001.

GRÖNROOS CHRISTIAN, Marknadsföring i tjänsteföretag. Elanders Graphic Systems AB, 1996. Sweden.

HUIZINGH, Eelko K.R.E. **Toward succesful electronic strategies: a hierarchy of three management models**. Disponível em: <www.ub.rug.nl/eldoc/som/99b45/99b45.pdf>. Acesso em: 19 ago. 2003.

KIM Dae-Young, LEHTO Y. Xinran; MORRISON M Alastair. Gender differences in online travel information search: implications for marketing communications on the internet. **Tourism Management**, v. 28, issue 2, pages 423-433, april 2007.

MALHOTRA, Naresh K. **Pesquisa de marketing:** uma orientação aplicada. 3. ed. Porto Alegre: Bookman, 2001.

MATTAR, Fauze Najib. **Pesquisa de marketing**. 2. ed. São Paulo: Atlas, 2000.

MATTAR, Fauze Najib. **Pesquisa de marketing:** metodologia, planejamento. São Paulo: Atlas, 1996.

MINAYO, Maria Cecília de Souza. **O desafio do conhecimento:** pesquisa qualitativa em saúde. 2. ed. São Paulo: HUCITEC; Rio de Janeiro:ABRASCO, 1993.

MONTGOMERY, Cynthia; PORTER, Michael. **Estratégia:** uma vantagem competitiva. 7. ed. Rio de Janeiro: Campus, 1998.

ORTEGA, Enrique; GONSALEZ, Ladislau. Marketing research in different settings. **Journal of Business Research**, v. 60, issue 2, pages 95-97, February 2007.

RICHARDSON, J. Roberto. **Pesquisa social, métodos e técnicas**. 2. ed. São Paulo: Atlas, 1999.

SOUMITRA, Dutta; SEGEV, Arie. Business transformation on the Internet. **European Management Journal**, v. 17, issue 5, p. 466-476, out. 1999.

SODRE, Ulisses Nunes. Onde Você Gostaria de Passar Suas Férias? **Revista Turismo**, ago. 2000. Disponível em: <http://revistaturismo.cidadeinternet.com.br/pesquisas/enquete1.htm>. Acesso em: 27 fev. 2007.

VARADARAJAN, Rajan P.; YADAV, Manjit S. Marketing strategy and the Internet: an organizing framework. **Journal of the Academy of Marketing Science**, v. 30, n. 4, p. 296-312, Fall 2002.

VIEIRA, Valter Afonso. As tipologias, variações e características da pesquisa de marketing. **Revista da FAE**, Curitiba, v. 5, n. 1, p. 61-70, jan./abr. 2002.

WORLD TOURISM ORGANIZATION, v. 5, n. 1, january 2007. Disponível em: <http://revistaturismo.cidadeinternet.com.br/negocios/mercadoturistico.htm>. Acesso em: 19 mar. 2007.

WIND, Yoram; MAHAJAN, Vijay. **Marketing de convergência:** estratégias para conquistar o novo consumidor. São Paulo: Pearson Education, 2003.

WRIGHT, Peter; KROLL, Mark J.; PARNEL, John. **Administração estratégica:** conceitos. São Paulo: Atlas, 2000.

Chapter Nine

Collaborative Arrangement Between Firms

A number of factors (Ito and Rose, 2004) speak for the need for most firms, in our globalize world, to seek collaborative arrangements with other firms, if survival and success in the increased competitive markets are of prime importance to them. As maintained by Doyle and Stern (2006), examples abound (e.g. General Motors, Marks and Spencer, General Electrics and Chrysler) of companies, which were once considered to be icons in their industries, but today, in the 21st century, are fighting for their survival. Hence, success in the rapidly changing markets can be a temporal phenomenon, if firms are not able to cope with changes that occur in the global village. Since no firm or organization has all the capabilities (e.g. resources, activities, and competencies) to achieve its goals or objectives (Prahalad and Håkansson and Snehota, 1995; Hamel, 1996; Awuah and Abraha, 2002) in the marketplace, most firms see it as an imperative to co-operate with other firms, sometimes even with competitors, so as to be able to leverage their capabilities. Essentially, a firm may have different co-operative arrangements with a number of other firms. The inter-firm co-operative arrangements can be joint development agreements, joint product development, co-operation in order to gain access to technologies, access to certain markets, alternative sourcing agreements, and joint ventures (Czinkota, M.R., and Ronkainen, I.A., 1998; Davies, W., and Brush, K.E., 1997; Prahalad and Hamel, 1996).

Once any firm realizes that alone it will be difficult to succeed and/or survive in the highly competitive markets, it will seek to establish some collaborative arrangements with other firms. This is because gaining access to certain external capacities will be crucial for the firm's success and survival. For Håkansson (1989), the total capacity of any firm will include its own internal capacity (i.e. own control of resources and/or activities) and external capacities (i.e. its indirect control of the resources and/or activities of other actors), to which the firm has access as the result of its exchange relationships (see also Håkansson and Snehota, 1995). There are some general motives or advantages for firms to have collaborative arrangements, as enumerated below:

- Spread and reduce costs or risks
- To block or co-opt or to avoid competition
- Gain market knowledge

Spread and reduce costs or risks

When the development and the commercialization of a product becomes very expensive and complex, for example, the costs and the risk of failure will be enormous for a single firm or even only two firms to bear (Czinkota and Ronkainen, 2007). Hence, it is not unusual to see that firms and even non-business organizations co-operate, using the strategic alliances arrangement, to bring about the success of the product, thus its development and commercialization (see e.g. Awuah and Abraha, 2002). As Czinkota and Ronkainen (2007, p. 190) assert, developing one pharmaceutical drug can take about 12 years, with competitive efforts close behind, and cost the company an annual R&D budget running to about $ 5 billion. Here, the authors maintain that only global products for global markets can support that much risk (p. 190). But, apart from establishing collaborative arrangements with a number of other actors in order to be able to develop and commercialize such a drug, entering other markets, other than the firm's own domestic market, the firm may enter into joint venture and licensing arrangements with other firms. For some firms, collaborative arrangements with other firms help them share risks with others (Beamish and Lu, 2004).

To block or co-opt or to avoid competition

Firms may enter into collaborative agreements with other firms in order to attack their own rivals. With the complementary resources and activities coming from a firm's partner, a firm will be able to co-opt its rivals. The Caterpillar and Mitsubishi's joint venture in Japan is an example of how Caterpillar, a heavy earth moving equipment producer, managed to strike back at its main global rival, Komatsu, in its home market (Czinkota and Ronkainen, 2007, p. 302). For others, they form a joint venture in order to avoid competition and leverage capabilities. The joint venture between SONY and Ericsson in the mobile phone market is one such an example. SONY and Ericsson had both been, before they joined forces, competing with each other in the mobile phone market. When the two realized that operating alone, each of them was not in the position to match the intense competition in the mobile phone market, they merged together. The strategic alliance between Microsoft and Intel has enabled them to dominate desktop computing (Ito and Rose, 2004). The two companies are said to have worked to increase their influence beyond the desktop computing market. By investing in or acquiring companies in a variety of associated business areas, including application software and hardware developers (audio, video, and web), various communication technology providers (cable, fiber optics, broadband, mobile, and satellite), and companies involved in enterprise networking, media, games, and PDA, (p. 77) Microsoft and Intel have become very strong in many markets.

Gain market knowledge

Collaborative arrangements are deeply ingrained in the principle that the partners complement each other in a number of areas. One such arrangement is how a firm will collaborate with other firms in order to get access to certain markets (Prahalad and Hamel, 1996; Beamish and Lu, 2004). NEC, a Japanese electronics provider, is said to have made a number of strategic alliances in order to be able to have market and technology access (Prahalad and Hamel, 1996, p. 124). Pharmacia, a Swedish pharmaceutical company, and Upjohn, an American pharmaceutical company, merged together to be able to complement each other when operating in the global market. Pharmacia's competence, at the time of the merger, was said to be in different technologies in the area of pharmacy and in market knowledge in Europe, while Upjohn's competence lay in other technologies in the area of pharmacy, which Pharmacia was lacking, and in market knowledge in the big U.S. market. Joining together, on November 2, 1995, Pharmacia and Upjohn could leverage each other's capabilities to be able to compete in the highly competitive pharmaceutical markets worldwide (Frankelius, 1999).

As reviewed above, collaborative arrangements between firms are very important for all firms, since no firm, acting alone, in the globalize markets can cope with the intense competition which globalization and trade liberalization create. If no firm is excluded from the search for co-operation with some other resourceful actors in the marketplace, then small, inexperienced, and less resourceful firms in Ghana or most firms in the Developing World may consider adopting the attitude of collaborating with some others so as to be able to leverage each other's capabilities, as they strive to cope with the challenges of globalization and the intense competition. Hence, we will discuss the motives or advantages and the difficulties of having the following specific collaborative arrangements: Joint venture, strategic alliances, and government consortia.

Joint ventures

A joint venture (JV) is a collaborative arrangement, which enables each of the partners to supplement its strengths (a firm can be weak in finance, market knowledge, technology, and human resources) with those of partners through co-operation (Dahringer, et al. 2006). A joint venture can be between two or more organizations, where the partners share assets, risks, and profits (Daniels and Radeburgh, 2001). Partners in a JV may hold equal shares, 50/50 or one partner may have the majority shares (Daniels and Radeburgh, 2001). JV can be used among firms within their domestic markets and also can be used when firms internationalize their businesses; it may help firms to enter foreign markets and the development of position in the foreign markets (Brassington and Pettitt, 2006). Indigenous firms in Ghana or other Developing Countries will stand to gain, if they begin, if they have not done it yet, to adopt the attitude of co-operating with others in order to meet increased competition, which they face in their domestic markets. Or they can even attempt to internationalize their businesses by entering into JV arrangements with some indigenous or foreign companies. As reported elsewhere (Ito and Rose, Deng, 2007), Chinese firms have been using JV arrangements and merger and acquisitions to strengthen their positions in internationalizing their businesses, especially in the industrial markets.

The JV between China's largest television manufacturer, TCL, and France's Thomson, a giant manufacturer of electronic products, resulted in a JV deal totalling $560 million. The TCL-Thomson Electronics' (TTE) JV, formed in July, 2004, enabled TCL to hold 67% stake in the JV, representing one of the largest agreements, in which a Chinese firm has taken control of a Western Company (Deng, 2007, p.76). TCL's position in the marketplace is described as follows:

> "The joint venture, TTE, gives TCL effective control of Thomson's television plants in France, Poland, and Thailand, making TCL the largest manufacturer of televisions globally. Covering all the world's major markets, this JV signifies the first step in TCL's effort to become China's first truly global corporation. While TTE enables TCL to circumvent non-trade barriers on the importation of Chinese television sets into Europe, TCL's primary motivation lies in taking advantage of Thomson's long-standing foothold in North America and Europe, and core proprietary technology such as RCA, owner of the well-recognized Nipper trademark" (Deng, 2007, p. 76).

Benefits with JV

By sharing competencies (the parties leverage each other's specialized competences), market knowledge and spreading and reducing costs among the partners, each of the partners will gain from the arrangement. Goal achievement in the marketplace, which when left to the efforts of one partner alone in the face of intense competition, could be difficult, can be realized as the partners complement each other (Czinkota and Ronkainen, 2007). Altogether, the partners are expected to have their respective unique advantages which will benefit the JV. There should, therefore, be a 'win-win' co-operation. JVs between foreign firms and domestic firms in a host country can facilitate relationships with local organizations (e.g. government, local authorities, or labour unions (Czinkota and Ronkainen, 2007, p. 301). But, unfortunately, there can be difficulties associated with JVs, as discussed below.

Problems with JVs

As reported in Daniels and Radeburgh (2001), half of JVs do break down. A number of reasons can be given for the difficulties associated with the successful implementation of JVs among firms. In the course of time, a partner or partners in the JV may view the importance of the JV differently. There could be lack of time to learn how to understand the other party and how its organization functions. The JV can also break because one or both parties feel it can now go alone (Brassington and Pettitt, 2006). This is especially the case when one party has the perception that it contributes more than the other partner (Daniels and Radeburgh, 2001). The failure of JV may also stem from the different objectives which the partners might have had before the formation of the JV. Control problems and different cultures may also be one of the reasons why the JV may break up.

"Major problems can arise due to conflicts of interest, problems with disclosure of sensitive information, and disagreement over how profits are to be shared; these are typically the result of a lack of communication and planning before, during, and after the formation of the venture" (Czinkota and Ronkainen, 2007, p. 301).

"Even with careful partner selection and explicit contractual agreements, the ever-changing business environment means that many joint ventures are plagued by problems related to the give and take among partner firms and issues of perceived fairness with respect to resources provided and returns received" (Ito and Rose, 2004, p. 76).

In summary, to make a JV work, the partners will have to be careful in selecting partners. They will have to have goal congruence or be flexible and be prepared to compromise when it comes to the need to address conflicting goals, for example. Adapting to each other will be needed to enable the partners to cope with the changing marketing conditions and other changes. The partners having shared and mutually understood objectives and also having long-term commitment will be crucial for the success of any JV (Dahringer et al., 2006).

Strategic alliances

"Strategic alliances play an important role in global strategies because it is common for a firm to lack a key success factor for a market. It may be distribution, a brand name, a sales organization, technology, R&D capability, or manufacturing capability. To remedy this deficiency internally might require excessive time and money. When the uncertainties of operating in other countries are considered, a strategic alliance is a natural alternative for reducing investment and the accompanying inflexibility and risks" (Aaker, 2001, p. 277).

In their discussion of the co-operations among firms, Ito and Rose (2004) assert that joint ventures traditionally involve a small number of partner firms, which co-operate to deal with specific business situations, such as marketing, production, R&D, or new market entry. However, in recent times especially, western firms have been using collaborative arrangements that are beyond the rather limited joint venture framework (Ito and Rose, 2004, p. 76). Firms are creating an emerging organizational structure, consisting of a large number of firms operating in a variety of different industries. A number of attempts have been made to define what a strategic alliance is (Aaker, 2001; Czinkota and Ronkainen, 2007;). Two of such definitions are worthy of note here.

According to Aaker (2001), a strategic alliance is a collaboration leveraging the strengths of two or more organizations to achieve strategic goals. For Czinkota and Ronkainen (1995, p. 283), strategic alliances are a manifestation of inter-organizational co-operative strategies that entail the pooling of skills and resources by the alliance partners in order to achieve one or more goals linked to the strategic objectives of the co-operating firms. While such definitions point to some important facts about strategic alliances, we need to add that it is imperative for firms to develop some kind of exchange relationships with some significant others as a means to gain access to activities and resources that they lack (Awuah Abraha, 2002). Studies elsewhere (Håkansson and Snehota, 1995; Håkansson et al, 2004) have proved that exchange relationships with some external actors are a necessity for most firms since they provide access to complementary resources and activities which may have an impact on their performance and/or success in the marketplace. Strategic alliances may take different forms.

Forms of strategic alliances

A strategic alliance can be a loose informal agreement, with no equity agreements for joint R&D, joint product development, long-term sourcing agreements, joint manufacturing, joint marketing, reciprocal, and distribution (Aaker, 2001; Dess, et al, 1994). This form of alliance, according to Aaker (2001), is fast and flexible to implement. The informal alliance can be adjusted as conditions and people change. The problem with this form, as posited by Aaker (2001, p. 278), is commitment. Since exit barriers are low and commitment is also low, the level of strategic importance is usually low; hence, there is a temptation for partners to back away or to disengage when difficulties arise.

The formal alliances, on the other hand, may include (Dess, et al, 1994, p. 4; Ito and Rose, 2004) equity agreements (e.g. joint venture, minority equity positions, and equity swaps). Moreover, a formal alliance involving equity and a comprehensive legal document has very different risks (Aaker, 2001).

"When equity sharing is involved, there is often worry about control, return on investment, and achieving a fair percentage of the venture. A major concern is whether such a permanent arrangement will be equitable in the face of uncertainty about the relative contributions of the partners and the eventual success of the endeavour" (Aaker, 2001, p. 278).

Other concerns may relate to lack of commitment and flexibility, a behaviour that might be ingrained in the partners' respective equity positions and the accompanying limits on each partner's contribution as conditions change. There is also the likelihood that the partners may rely excessively on legal documents to preserve the health of the alliance (p. 278). These are worthy of note for all firms that might have the desire to go into an alliance with others, for alliances have benefits, if partners can handle them to mutual benefits. We will, therefore, look into the motives for strategic alliances.

Goals or motivations for the formation of strategic alliances

The alliance partners can pool their resources and strengths together in order to achieve their respective goals, something that would have been impossible for each of the partners to achieve if they were to work separately. Here, the formal alliance partners may also draw on their relationships with third parties (non-formal members of the alliance) to leverage capabilities that will help the formal partners achieve their goals. When Scanditronix Medical Share Company (SMSC), a Swedish small-sized company, needed to develop advanced radiotherapy systems, technically and clinically, SMSC built alliances with the University of Rochester (URU) in the U.S.A. (mainly working with a doctor doing research at this university), Doctor Daniel Den Hoed Clinic in Holland (DDHCH), and Hitachi Medical Corporation (HMC) in Japan, the three partners forming formal alliances. However, the SMSC, DDHCH and SMC alliance partners had to co-operate with a number of non-formal members (e.g. hospitals in Sweden, U.S., Holland, and Japan) of the alliance to develop and commercialize advanced radiotherapy systems (Awuah and Abraha, 2002). The strategic alliance in question enabled the partners to play a leading role in the development of radiotherapy systems in the world as a whole. The alliance members have been developing new positions in their own networks and in the networks of their respective partners (p. 691). Hence, alliances may facilitate a firm's entry into global markets and/or expand its markets across different borders.

The Japanese firm, JVC, was able to provide VCR design and manufacturing capability but needed a relationship with Thompson to obtain help in accessing the fragmented European market (Aaker, 2001, p. 278). Strategic alliances allow the partners to spread costs and risks (Aaker, 2001; Awuah and Abraha, 2002). As Aaker (2001) reports, the fixed investment that Toyota made in designing a car and its production system is now spread over more units because of a joint venture with GM in California. Strategic alliances may also help partners to overcome trade barriers. There are several other motives for forming alliances (Hyder and Abraha, 1999). However, as briefly mentioned above, strategic alliances may also have some risks.

Some of the risks consist in the partners' inability to carefully evaluate the effects of forming strategic alliances. The partners may not have good knowledge of each other and their respective objectives. Moreover, a partner may behave opportunistically (Awuah and Abraha, 2002, p. 681). To overcome risks and avoid failures in strategic alliance, a partner may have to (1) carefully select and evaluate its partner(s), (2) the partners may have a commonality of orientation and/or goals, (3) the partners may have to bring into the alliance complementary and relevant benefits; the alliance will be of less benefit if both partners have expertise in the same area, and (4) the partners will have to carefully deal with differences in organizations, people, cultures, structures, and systems in country cultures (Awuah and Abraha, 2002; Dess, et al, 1994). All in all, the extent to which firms are using strategic alliances today to achieve various goals, as the examples below illustrate, warrant that Ghanaian firms, for example, may have to cast a wide net into their business environment and seek collaborative arrangements with some resourceful partners. One area, which also needs be discussed, is strategic alliances that are known as government consortia.

Government consortia

It is not unusual for governments to actively step in to contribute to collaborative arrangements between firms. As reported elsewhere (Ito and Rose, 2004; Beamish and Lu, 2004) Japanese and Chinese governments actively sponsor collaborative ventures which are deemed to be of national interest; this is because such alliances are perceived to boost the competitiveness of firms.

"A wide range of cooperative R&D mechanisms were employed by U.S. industry. Most collaborative projects involve joint activity without direct government involvement. Moreover, participation in joint R&D is initiated for many reasons. Greater competition from innovative foreign producers, for example, has prompted some U.S. companies to seek the technological synergies of industry-wide cooperation. Other motives include the desire to lower R&D costs, to monitor the capabilities of rival firms, and to learn state-of-the-art manufacturing techniques" (Reports on Government Consortia, 1998).

As Czinkota and Ronkainen maintain (2007), the escalating costs in research and development of certain strategic technologies or products (e.g. a new drug, computer or telecommunication switch) may underlie a government's motive to co-operate with or even subsidize certain firms to bring a product into the marketplace. To overcome high costs and risks or research and development, research consortia have merged in the United States, Japan, and Europe (Czinkota and Ronkainen, 2007, p. 302). The challenges of globalization, increased opportunities and threats, are far beyond any single government or a firm. Hence, all over the world, nations (e.g. firms in them) must invest in breeding actors who will be able to cope with the challenges of globalization by bringing innovative solutions which are new and better than the existing ones. Since competitors upgrade their concepts, use new ways of doing things and/or are innovative in new solutions, with or without government active support, firms that do not embark on upgrading their ways of doing things, through innovations, may be out-competed. This is what has been happening to most firms in Ghana and in many developing countries. However, as the foregoing discussions have shown, the 'go alone' strategy to deal with the challenges posed by globalization is not tenable. A government or a firm will need to forge collaborative arrangements with many others whose resources and activities may complement one's own. In a consortium, the interacting actors pool their resources for research into technologies ranging from artificial intelligence and electric car batteries to semiconductor manufacturing (Czinkota and Ronkainen(2007, p. 303).

Summary

In summary, the main thrust of this chapter has been to highlight the fact that no single firm and even government is self-sufficient enough to be able to achieve its goal if one adopts the 'go alone strategy'. By forging collaborative arrangements with other actors (firms, government, and private individuals), the members, by co-operating with each other, will be able to, among other things, leverage their capabilities where the sharing of knowledge, experiences and other complementary resources will be common rather than exceptional. Since there are many collaborative arrangements, with benefits and problems, any form of collaborative arrangement (joint venture, formal and informal strategic alliances, and government consortia) would need to be carefully designed or formed and well-run to enable the partners to achieve goals which would have been impossible if each of them had operated alone. The merits and demerits of the various forms of collaborative arrangements, as discussed above, can serve as guidelines for any firm or government that aspires to forge collaborative arrangements with some other significant actors in its environment. They are not exhaustive, so there is room to find what more can add to the benefits or the problems for co-operating with others and then select and use the form that best suits your motives and goals.

References

Aaker, D. A. (2001). *Strategic Market Management*. (6th ed.). New York: John Wiley & Sons, Inc.

Awuah, G. B., and Abraha, D. (2002). Inter-organizational Co-operation: a New View of Strategic Alliances. The case of Swedish firms in the international market, Industrial *Marketing Management* 31, pp. 679-693.

Beamish, P.W, and Lu, J. W. (2004). Network Development and Firm Performance: A Field Study of Internationalizing Japanese Firms. *The Multinational Business Review*, Vol. 12, No. 3 (Winter), pp. 41-61.

Brassington, F. and Pettitt, S. (2006). *Principles of Marketing*. (4th Ed.). Edinburgh Gate: Pearson Education Limited.

Czinkota, M.R., and Ronkainen, I. A. (2007). *International Marketing* (8 Ed.), United States of America. Thomson South-Western.

Czinkota, M.R. and Ronkainen, I.A. (1995). *International Marketing*. (4th Ed.). New York: Dryden Press.

Czinkota, M.R. and Ronkainen, I.A. (1998). *International Marketing*. (5th Ed). New York: Dryden Press.

Dahringer, L., Leihs, H, and Mühlbacher, H. (2006). *International Marketing- A Global Perspective*, (3rd. Ed.). London: Thomson Learning.

Daniels and Radebaugh, (2001). *International Business: Environments and Operations*, 9th Edition, Prentice-Hall, London.

Davies, W., and Brush, K.E. (1997). High-tech. Industry Marketing: the Elements of a Sophisticated Global Strategy. *Ind Mark Manage* 26, pp. 1-13.

Deng, P. (2007). Investing for Strategic Resources and Its Rationale: The Case of Outward FDI from Chinese Companies. *Business Horizons* 50, pp. 71-81.

Dess, G., Walter, B.A, and Peters, S. (1994). Strategic Alliances and Joint Ventures: Making Them Work. *Business Horizon* 5-10 (July – August).

Frankelius, P. (1999). *Pharmacia & Upjohn. Erfarenheter från ett världsföretags utveckling. Företagande över tid*, Volymn II, Doctoral Dissertation, Internationell Handelskolan, Jönköping: Liber Ekonomi.

Hamel, G. and Prahalad, C.K. (1996). *Competing for the Future*. Boston: Harvard Business School Press.

Håkansson, H., Harrison, D., and Waluszewski, A. (2004). *Rethinking Marketing: Developing a New Understanding of Markets*. Chichester. John Wiley & Sons Ltd.

Håkansson, H. and Snehota, I. (1995). *Developing Relationships in Business Networks*. London: Routledge.

Håkansson, H. (1989). *Corporate Technological Behaviour: Co-operation and Networks*. London: Routledge.

Hyder, S-A and Abraha, D. (1999). Product and Skills Development in Small- and Medium-sized High-tech Firms through International Strategic Alliances. Global Business in the Age of Technology. *Eighth Annual World Business Conference Proceedings*. June 30-July 3. Monterey, CA. USA: International Management Development Association, pp. 133-141.

Ito. K. and Rose, E.L. (2004). An Emerging Structure of Corporations. *The Multinational Business Review*. Vol. 12 No. 3. (Winter 2004). pp. 63-83.

Report on Government Consortia (1998), available at: http://books.nap.edu/openbok.php?record_id=1998&page=193. (Accessed November 18, 2007).

Chapter Ten

Carving The Way Towards A Successful And Sustainable Development

In the light of the various discussions provided in the previous chapters and in line with the current Ghana government's ambition to make Ghana a middle-income country by the year 2015, we dedicate this concluding chapter to the immediate areas which need to be prepared now for Ghana to be in the race to provide sustainable growth that will translate into jobs for the masses and thereby increase their income.

Identify and develop critical projects

There will be the need for government, industry and places of learning to join forces, by forming a particular consortium comprising experts from the three stakeholders to work around a specific project, which can be of relevance in many areas. For example, the Japanese government-sponsored consortium, to bring about the Fifth Generation Computer Project in artificial intelligence, has fuelled the U.S. to support and sponsor its own comparable consortia. The U.S has formed a consortium, The Microelectronics and Computer Technology Corporation (MCC). MCC are companies, in consortium, that concentrate on application-oriented hardware and software R&D in the electronic sector (Report on Government Consortia, 1998). Evidently, members or stakeholders in the Japanese, or in the U.S., consortium working on specific projects will have, throughout their respective project's lifetime, close and regular interaction where they leverage each other's capabilities in achieving their goals.

It is very essential that the representatives of academia, industry and government have a clearly formulated project to which each organization (and their representatives) will bring complementary and relevant benefits. The idea generation and its development into some tangible or intangible solution, from the consortium, might be of use in many areas. One classic example is the electronic technology. A Singaporean's view of how that country's investment in the area of the electronic industry helped the country immensely is captured in the quotation below:

> "In a sense, the benefits the ASEAN-3 (and any other Third World country) can obtain from taking part in the thriving world electronics industry result from the special characteristics of the industry. The main features, in addition to fast growth of market size, include rapid advances in technology, and applications of its products to many fields. Apart from computers, consumer electronics such as TV sets, video and audio systems, electronic systems take up a large part of the total output of aviation and defence products, communications equipment, machine tools and industrial control systems. In turn, each of these electronic products makes use of many components and subassemblies in production" (Swee, 1995, p. 342).

Singapore's national investment in the electronic technology, with its attendant applications in many fields, produced the following results:

> "The annual Census of Industrial Production showed that between 1978 and 1989, the output of electronic products, measured in terms of value added, increased from US$362 million to US$3,604 million. As a proportion of total manufacturing output, this represented an increase of 15.8% in 1978 to 35.6% in 1989. Employment increased from 47,455 to 115,837, representing 19.3% and 34.2% of manufacturing workforce. What is notable is the increase in value added per worker, US$7.6 thousand in 1978 to US$31.1% thousand in 1989" (Swee, 1995, pp. 342-343).

Even though the Singapore's example may seem to be a little old, it is in line with what the U.S. and the Japanese have been doing over the years, identifying technological fields that can be harnessed to boost the competitiveness of firms in many areas. The recent examples of the respective consortia they sponsor say it all. The Chinese government is also said to actively identify and finance Chinese firms to make foreign direct investments through mergers and acquisitions in highly advanced countries to gain access to technologies which they lack in China (Beamish and Lu, 2004).

Right now, most Ghanaian-made goods (Awuah, 2005) are considered to be inferior compared to their competing alternatives from foreign producers (see also Chapter Six, the nail producers in Ghana). Hence, consumers will opt for foreign products, leaving Ghanaian firms to incur loses and eventually go out of business. Chapter Three and Six provide evidences of the inability of Ghanaian firms to compete in the face of intense competition from finished products from abroad. Ghanaian firms, with their brands, need to struggle very hard to develop quality images as the result.

The use of modern technology such as computer aided design, computer aided manufacturing, and sophisticated packaging that reinforces the aesthetics of advanced design are all lacking among many Ghanaian firms. When a society is able to adopt a particular technology which has a wider application and utilize it very well, as the Singapore experience has shown, productivity or growth increases and employment also increases. Since the capital base of the Ghanaian state is small and each individual firm is also small, many small entrepreneurs identifying common interests and pooling complementary resources from some identifiable actors (e.g., the government, firms, private individuals, and places of higher learning) might make it possible for them to co-operate in exploiting some meaningful technologies that could be used by many actors in many sectors. The capital and the infrastructure to help people research and develop meaningful technologies would be too high a cost and risk for a single actor to bear. Hence, collective efforts would be needed, as have been emphasized throughout this book.

In areas where a single actor can learn, build its own infrastructure to use a new technology, and develop the technology over time, as the La Palm

Beach's example in Chapter Eight seems to show, that needs to be commended; and we should encourage other firms to emulate that. This is essential because the pace of technological changes in areas such as the information technology (I.T technology), the Internet and the e-post can enable a firm in the U. S. or anywhere in the world to reach and serve customers anywhere on the globe from the firm's (the seller) home market. This development implies that as competition in our open markets increases, customers have increased varieties of goods/services to choose from and can select to do business with the firm that provides 'total benefits' to satisfy the customer's needs better than competitors can. For any firm, therefore, the challenge will be the ability to satisfy these increased, multidimensional demands of scale, scope, and speed, according to Ito and Rose (2004), which the technological developments bring with them, on its own. For Ito and Rose (2004, p.77), the often-conflicting imperatives may be more readily met by combining the resources of multiple organizations.

Where the need to join other firms in a joint venture arrangement, a strategic alliance, and/or in consortia with several others, in order to develop a new product, technology or whatever that will boost their respective competitiveness, firms do not have to hesitate in responding to that opportunity. And in a society like Ghana, the government will have to be very pro-active in identifying and supporting firms, especially through consortia arrangements, that have the potentiality to cope with the intense global competition, for the global competition leaves no country and or firm untouched. For firms to be able to upgrade their technologies, business processes, and their IT technologies, which will enable them to effectively interact and serve the needs of customers who are faced with an abundance of alternative solutions/substitutes, employees may have to constantly undergo career training and/or competence development. Here forging co-operation with universities and other places of higher learning will be of much help. As Lundvall (1992) maintains, learning is a social activity, which involves interaction between people. Dwelling on studies made elsewhere (Awuah, 2007; Tzokas & Saren, 2004), an organization's capability to learn and perform better is complemented by its capability to engage in mutual learning with actors with whom the organization interacts. There are studies that stress the fact that collaboration between universities and companies when effectively utilized will be of mutual benefits to the partners (Starbuck, 2001; Hadjimanolis, 2006; Tucker, 2007).

For example, co-operation with universities will enable a firm to gain access to modern science, new technologies, and innovative processes, which, when learned and adopted, may boost the firm's competitiveness. The university researchers, on the other hand, may also learn from companies, since the latter provide practical knowledge concerning the usefulness and the scope of new knowledge, technology or innovation, which the parties have developed together. What needs be stressed here is the potential inherent in the collaboration between universities and companies. Many governments and companies are aware of this potential so they provide funds to help universities-companies' product development, innovation processes, and knowledge generation and dissemination that may help in local, regional and national development (Lundvall, 1992; Tucker, 2007). Thus, companies can donate funds for research involving universities and companies; similarly, governments may fund research collaboration between universities and certain companies. In their efforts to have Nordic Joint Investments in several development areas, the Prime Ministers of the Nordic countries, during their June 2007 meeting, made a strong point concerning the need to compete for talents and innovations.

> "Globalization means that research and education are internationalized and that the competition for talents and innovations becomes intensive" (Göteborgs Posten, October 28, 2007: 63).

The above quotation can be likened to what Prahalad and Hamel (1996) emphasized. Thus, tomorrow's growth will depend on today's competence building. The search for people with the talents and skills to bring about innovative solutions in a society should go on unabated.

A future industry or market, which the whole world is eager to see that it takes off in full swing, develop and be sustained, is the renewable energy market. This is a market which has the potential to save the world from the dangers of greenhouse gases which cause global warming with its attendant catastrophes (e.g. the heating up of our environments). The renewable energy may also have the potential to bring many jobs into areas that can develop and commercialize renewable energy sources. The current energy sources, for example, fossil fuel (such as coal and oil) pose environmental threats. The high emissions of carbon dioxide (CO_2), which is the cause of greenhouse effect and global warming mostly come from the use of fossil fuels. Hence, many actors (nations, governments, and firms) are in search of the technologies, the capital, and the 'will' to invest in renewable energy sources such as energy or power from water, wind, sunshine, and biomass. Hence, in countries such as Ghana, investing in renewable energy sources should be a priority. Most of the current energy sources pose a threat to long-term development.

"Burning fossil fuels is a major cause of air pollution and increases the accumulation of greenhouse gasses in the upper atmosphere, which may already be causing global warming.

Weizmann Institute scientists are concerned about this state of affairs and a number of them have recently made commitments to help search for solutions" (Report on Renewable Energy, 2007).

The recent discovery of oil reserves in Ghana, not yet harnessed, is a blessing for the country and those who are rejoicing over that opportunity are right in doing that. But, the future of the country as far as its energy needs, their development and commercialization, are concerned, depends on the extent to which the diversification of the sources of energy, where renewable ones dominate, is carried on through time. The investment in developing and commercializing renewable energy has the greatest potentiality to generate growth and jobs in the future, as most of the countries in the world are looking for better energy sources which are clean, efficient and have virtually no negative effects on the environment.

Alone, no single actor will be able to make any significant investment in all or even any of the renewable energy sources mentioned above. But, by pooling resources (knowledge, skills, and capital) from several actors (foreigners and indigenous people), some future renewable energy market(s), with its windows of opportunities, could be developed and run for the benefit of all (firms, organizations, and private individuals). Once the whole world is involved in the search for alternative energy sources, because most of the current energy sources are not sustainable in the long run due to dangers they pose, seeking collaborative arrangements with actors beyond one's own country to invest together in renewable energy sources becomes important. On Monday, December 3, 2007, representatives from190 countries met in a conference in Bali to discuss and to agree to limit the emission of green house gases, which affects our environment very negatively (Dagens Industri, Monday 3 December, 2007: 2). Already many countries have signed the Kyoto Agreement, which seeks to have the countries to reduce the emission of carbon dioxide by 5 percent between 2008 and 2012. Still the world wants to do more to save the environment by reaching a new agreement with all countries to agree to reduce substantially the emission of carbon dioxide into the atmosphere.

One important development, which this increased awareness of the harm the fossil fuels cause, is the challenge for the world economies to reduce their use or consumption of fossil fuels (e.g. oil). This advice to reduce oil consumption may not come well for the countries whose economies are very much dependent on the exploitation and sale of oil. But we all have to save our planet, so even the Organization of Petroleum Exporting Countries (OPEC), the major exporters of oil, are also advised to diversify their economies, reducing their dependence on oil in the long run (Dagens Industri, Monday 3 December, 2007: 2). This scenario of the world stressing the need to reduce oil consumption now and in the future should be a lesson for countries such as Ghana, which have newly discovered oil reserves. Of course, production of oil will still, in the short term benefit Ghana; but in the long term, diversifying its energy sources will be very crucial because potential buyers of fuels may be asking for renewable ones. Hence, future investments in the energy sector will have to consider diversifying the sector where renewable energy sources become very important.

Breeding and supporting modern entrepreneurship

"Few of the people who built fast food empires ever attended college, let alone business school. They worked hard, took risks, and followed their own paths" (Schlosser, E., 2002, p. 6).

As discussed in Chapters Three and Six, the emergence of some Ghanaian entrepreneurs are similar to those entrepreneurs that have revolutionized the fast food industry throughout the world. But there is one great difference which needs be reiterated again. It is the difference in working within an enabling environment or in an uncongenial environment. As Schlosser (2002, p. 33) reported, the founders of fast food chains in the U. S. could provide an overall corporate vision and grasp the public mood, relying on others to handle the creative and financial details. It is even said that Walt Disney neither wrote nor drew the animated classics that bore his name (Schlosser, E., 2002, p.33). The U. S. has the overall infrastructure: a well-educated labour force, the use of modern science and technology in many sectors, efficient transportation, communication, banking and financial systems. The likelihood for an emerged entrepreneur to have help (Ito and Rose, 2004) in the form of venture capital, technical knowledge, market knowledge, and forming alliances is very high in an enabling environment such as that of the U. S. The same cannot be said about entrepreneurs in Ghana; the evidences provided in Chapters Three and Six show this fact clearly.

Although the salaries in Africa are cheap, the disadvantage in doing business on the continent consists of poor infrastructure and transportation costs, factors which make products from Africa very expensive (Spiegel Special, 2007: 139). These factors are, among others, also mentioned as factors contributing to the high costs of doing business in Ghana (FIAS, 2003). Coupled with these problems, many Ghanaian entrepreneurs still use old technologies and practices which result in their low productivity and low market shares vis-à-vis their foreign competitors.

Customers that have the purchasing power and have become demanding and sophisticated when it comes to satisfying their needs, will not buy Ghanaian goods or services that are expensive and deemed as inferior. The liberalized Ghanaian market has made it possible for goods/services from foreign producers to flood the market. The foreign competition, mostly in the form of imported goods/services, is driving indigenous firms away from the market. For example, the 'street fast food culture' in Ghana has remained unchanged with regard to its preparation and delivery. Well-travelled and well-to-do Ghanaians, as well as foreigners, may be looking for the modern way of preparing and delivering fast food. Chapter Three and Six also provide examples of other areas where Ghanaian firms fall short in upgrading their methods and practices of helping customers meet their needs. But, the plain truth is that customers everywhere will choose to do business with suppliers or sellers that help meet their total needs (i.e. offering quality products, services, and competitive prices). Therefore, government, academia, and industry will need to help spot entrepreneurs and effectively help to upgrade their technologies and ways of doing business, and to help them gain access to affordable bank loans. And above all, they must operate in an environment where there are effective means of regular power supply, transportation and communication systems.

Foreign inputs and their contribution to growth

The challenge for every country to reduce poverty is a well-debated topic everywhere. Poverty reduction, as this book and other studies have revealed (Harrison, 1993; World development Report, 1990, 1994; Human Development Report, 2004), would greatly benefit any nation because it leads to viable economic exchanges between many producers and a large number of buyers who need goods and services to satisfy their needs. It is, therefore, essential that every nation such as Ghana tries to develop nation-wide socio-economic infrastructure that would facilitate the exchange relationships between all economic agents in the society.

Ghana's efforts to combat mass poverty by reducing the disparities between the poor and the non-poor in the cities and the rural areas have been going on since the country attained its independence from the British colonial rulers, who left an underdeveloped infrastructure when they relinquished control to Ghanaians (Ghana Exporters' Directory, 1991; Roe, 1991; Ghana: Handbook of Commerce and Industry, 1988/89; Todaro, 1994). However, the means used by Ghana to reduce poverty have been inadequate. The country is still heavily dependent on primary products as the major means to create the national wealth. Unfortunately, job generation and income generation for the masses are not coming from the primary sectors, namely, cocoa production, gold, diamond, bauxite, and manganese mining. This mono-culture, as the engine to Ghana's economic growth, has been a major concern for decades (Ghana Exporters' Directory, 1991; Roe, 1991). The agricultural sector still uses old technologies and tools, as the quote below shows.

> "Accra, Nov. 22, GNA - Professor Ivan Addae-Mensah, former Vice-Chancellor of the University of Ghana, on Thursday said Ghana had been at a "scientific standstill"

over the past 50 years, and called for a change in the national development policy.

> "Before Independence, our farmers were cultivating with cutlasses and hoes manufactured by our local blacksmiths, 50 years after independence our farmers are still farming with cutlasses and hoes imported from China, Europe and the Americas" (Development Debate, 2007).

The need to broaden Ghana's industrial capacity, however, has been a top development agenda item, as Chapter Two has shown. This has made succeeding governments of Ghana resort to going after foreign inputs as an essential factor in the socio-economic development of Ghana.

One of the foreign inputs, which Ghana has been using excessively over the years, is the taking of loans from the IMF, the World Bank, and other foreign banks (Akwetey, 1994; Svenska Dagbladet, January 18, 1989:4; Der Spiegel 35/1989:142). Unfortunately, the industrial capacity to absorb and use these foreign inputs and loans has been non-existent or under-developed. Ghana has been, in the millennium, classified as one of the highly indebted poor countries in the world. The country's admittance into the club of the Highly Indebted Poor Countries (HIPC) Initiative earned Ghana, as declared by its president, 7 billion dollars debt cancellation (Development Debate, 2007).

What has gone wrong with the country's industrial capacity building then? It appears that the indigenous resources (both human and natural) do not exist at all. Foreign aid, not loans, which the country has also been receiving over the years, has had insignificant impact on the country's development or growth. A concerned Ghanaian lamented over the fact that Ghana has not been able to change its economic structure in 40 years, with the result that the country still relies heavily on the export on raw materials and on foreign donors and development partners to fund her development budgets (Development Debate, 2007).

The Spiegel Special (2007, p. 148) offers a very disturbing analysis of African countries' inability to absorb and use foreign loans or development help to enhance their economic development. Most African countries have had no success with loans or development help. Although it is reported that the international development help to Africa doubled from 17.4 billion dollars in 1990 to 34.3 billion in 2004, Africa's contribution to the world trade has been insignificant. Africa, south of the Sahara, has 13 percent of the world's population, but the continent's contribution to the global economic trade is one or two percent. And among the 39 poorest countries in the world, 30 of them are in Africa (Spiegel Special, 2007, p. 148).

Ghana's experience with loans and foreign development help is reflected in the above 'depressing' picture of Africa. We, therefore, have suggested throughout this book, that African countries and their governments, particularly Ghana, should not fail to see the complementary relationships between foreign inputs and a country's own indigenous resources. Unfortunately, most countries in Africa have neglected the importance of involving as many actors as possible in a country's development, instead allowing only a few urban political elites (Human Development Report, 2004) to dominate development decisions.

"Economic austerity programmes have often been used to advantage by the ruling elites. And the dismantling of significant parts of the public sector, which market-oriented reforms usually require, without first creating a true market, has recentralized power in many cases. In that sense the structural adjustments of the 1980s and 1990s might be said to have had similar outcomes to the nationalizations of the 1960s and 1970s" (Human Development Report, 2004: 97).

There is no wonder that much loans and development help into many African countries have been misdirected, resulting in no progress. This is because, as reflected in the above quote, the development of many African countries, particularly Ghana, has become the monopoly of a few ruling elites. But preparing for a better tomorrow would demand that many actors be given the chance to contribute to the development of their country. The last important foreign input, which needs be discussed, is to have foreign direct investors (FDI) come to a country to do business, instead of importing finished products into a host-country.

FDI can play a major role in a country's development as has been shown in several studies (Economist June 20, 2001:2; Daniels and Radebaugh, 2001; Griffin, et al, 1998). For example, China's current strong position as the fourth largest export country in the world trade, after the U. S., Japan, and Germany, is partly explained by the contribution of foreign direct investors into the country. Half of China's exports are said to be produced by foreign firms (Dagens Industri, Wednesday May 5, 2004: 15). And in the ASEAN (South East Asian) area, it is reported that multinational companies (MNC) have been very instrumental in the development and/or growth, especially of the ASEAN – 3's (Singapore, Malaysia, and Thailand), export development (Swee, 1995, pp.331-351).

But, the competition for FDI, as discussed in Chapter Four, has shown that Ghana has not been successful in winning and sustaining many FDI as desired or expected. Most of the few FDI which Ghana has been able to attract and retain in recent times have all gone to the mining industries (Asante et al, 2000). A very insignificant number of FDI seemed to have invested in other sectors, such as manufacturing, component, high-tech industries, and energy. Hence, attempts to attract FDI into such sectors in the future should be a priority of policy makers.

The current strategy which countries have been using to attract significant number of FDI, as reported in Williams and Wint (2002), is a country's ability to have a strong per capita-income and economic growth on a continuous basis. Although a country's incentive structures or promotional activities, and the availability of raw materials may still play a role in attracting some FDI, for a significant and a diversified number of FDI to flow into a country, economic growth and a strong per capita-income are very crucial (Dagens Industri, Wednesday, May 5, 2004:15; Williams and Wint, 2002). Other factors of importance are the state of a country's infrastructure and policy framework. A country's policy framework is an important means to measure the level of risks in doing business in a particular host-country market. In the 1970s, Fieldhouse (1978, p. 601) remarked that any FDI's performance in most developing countries would not be determined so much by the firm's own strategies, but rather by government policies and how they are implemented. Hence, firms were advised to be very particular about government policy and the way it was implemented by the bureaucracy (Fieldhouse, 1978, p. 601).

In modern times, Ghana is among those countries where corruption is still widespread. In the Transparency International's Corruption Index, which was published in 2006, countries that had no corruption scored 10 points, where very corrupt countries scored 0 points. Ghana, Egypt, and Senegal, scored 3.3 points each (See Spiegel Special, 2007, p. 133). Paying bribes to corrupt bureaucrats are costs of doing business which cannot be accounted for in any accounting book (Awuah, 2005). Ghana's poorly developed infrastructure makes costs of doing business in the country very high (FIAS, 2003), so there should not be any room for additional costs, such as paying bribes to corrupt bureaucrats because that too will increase the costs of doing business. Below are the listed scores of Ghana with regard to the Corruption Perception Index (CPI), showing Ghana's position in relation to other countries in the world as well as to countries in Africa. The position of Ghana is not something to be proud of; corruption needs to be eradicated.

Corruption Perception Index 'Progress Report'

Year	Rank/World	Rank/Africa	CPI Score
2007	69/179	8/52	3.7
2006	70/163	4/44	3.3
2005	65/159	6/44	3.5
2004	65/146		3.6
2003	72/133		3.3
2002			3.9 (BEST)
2001			3.4
2000			3.5
1999			3.3

Explanatory notes

* CPI Score relates to perceptions of the degree of corruption as seen by business people and country analysts and ranges between **10 (highly clean) and 0 (highly corrupt)**.

Source: CPI Report (2007)

Since the competition for FDI is a global undertaking, countries such as Ghana should offer an enabling environment which would be competitive compared with those of its rivals. As Williams and Wint (2002) have found out, many developing countries' economic policies and promotional activities are converging to the point that they lose their comparative advantages. Thus, economic policies and promotional activities in almost all developing countries have become a "commodity", meaning they are all the same with no possibility to see any significant difference among them. A country must, therefore, be able to differentiate itself from the other rivals competing for FDI. What now counts are high growth, high per-capita income (with an increased middle income class), and a well-developed infrastructure. China, India, and Malaysia, for example, are attractive now for FDI because of their continuously high growth, high per capita income and well-developed infrastructure and government's positive attitude towards foreign investors (Dagens Industri, Wednesday October 20, 2004:17).

Finally, another area of importance is to encourage indigenous firms to enter into joint ventures, strategic alliances, or consortia among themselves or with some potential foreign direct investors. Since these collaborative arrangements would help foreign direct investors to share risks and costs, the propensity for them to be attracted to Ghana to invest would also be increased. China even goes to the extent of actively financing promising Chinese firms to merge or acquire firms in developed countries, which enables the Chinese firms to gain access to technologies, know-how, and markets (Ito and Rose, 2004; Beamish and Lu, 2004). Since most Chinese firms are struggling to upgrade their technologies and brand images vis-á-vis competitors from the developed world, they see great benefits in collaborating among themselves and with foreign partners. Governments and firms in developing countries, such as Ghana, will have nothing to lose by copying practices that seem to work elsewhere.

Collaborative arrangements among Ghanaian firms, which appear to be non-existent, may also help them leverage each other's capabilities and enable them compete in the dynamic and globalize markets of today. In most sectors in Ghana we have seen how many Ghanaian firms go out of business as soon as foreign competitors make inroads into. Collaborating with partners that bring into the co-operation complementary resources (e.g. diverse know-how, capital and contact networks) will help boost each of the partners' competitiveness in the marketplace.

And above all, the effective socio-economic and political policies, which will foster sustainable growth and equitable distribution of wealth, should have inputs from a group of actors that may constitute a 'think tank' that studies and analyzes trends, changes (e.g. technologies, demography, environment, and rules and regulations), and needs (of society, organization, and private individuals) in the environment. The contribution from a 'think tank' may go a long way to help identify opportunities in a dynamic society and suggest ways to exploit them. Analogously, a 'think tank' may also help identify threats stemming from the changes going on in a society and suggest ways to combat them. However, a 'think tank' is not to be seen as the sole body in a society to come up with suggestions regarding where opportunities will open up and how to exploit them. A 'think tank's contribution is complementary to the contributions from the rest of the people in a society, for the development of a country is a collective effort.

References

Akwetey, E. (1994). *Trade Unions and Democratization: A Comprehensive Study of Zambia and Ghana*, Dissertation, Department of Political Science, University of Stockholm, Stockholm.

Asante, Y., Gyasi, E.M., and Tsikata, G.K (2000). *Determinants of Foreign Direct Investment in Ghana.* Overseas Development Institute, Portland House, Stage Place, London SW1E 5DP.

Awuah, G, B. (2007). A Professional Services Firm's Competence Development. Industrial *Marketing Management* 36, pp. 1068-1081.

Awuah, G, B. (2005). *As I journey Along: A Ghanaian's Perception of Life in the Diaspora*. U.S.A. Lulu Press

Beamish, P.W, and Lu, J. W. (2004). Network Development and Firm Performance: A Field Study of Internationalizing Japanese Firms. *The Multinational Business Review*, Vol. 12, No. 3 (Winter), pp. 41-61.

CPI Report (2007), available at: http://www.ghanaweb.com/GhanaHomePage/NewsArchive/artikel.php?ID =134627: (Accessed November 22, 2007)

Dagens Industri, Wednesday, May 5, 2004:15

Dagens Industri, Wednesday, October 20, 2004:17

Dagens Industri, Monday, December 3, 2007: 2

Daniels and Radebaugh, (2001), *International Business: Environments and Operations,* 9th Edition, Prentice-Hall, London.

Development Debate (2007), Debate on some development paths taken in Ghana, available at: http://www.ghanaweb.com/GhanaHomePage/NewsArchives/artikel.php?ID=119493: (Accessed, February 2, 2007)

Der Spiegel 35/1989:142

Economist, June 20, 2001:42

FIAS (2003). *Ghana: Administrative Barriers to Investment Update*, Accra.

Fieldhouse, D.K. (1978). *"Unilever Overseas" – The Anatomy of a Multinational*, 1895-1965, London , Croom-Helm.

Ghana Exporters' Directory, (1991). Worldwide Press Limited, Accra.

Ghana: *Handbook of Commerce and Industry*, (1988/89). Ministry of Trade and Tourism, Accra.

Griffin, R., Mahoney, D., Pustay, M., Trigg, M, (1998). *International Business*, Longman, South Melbourne, Australia.

Göteborgs Posten, October 28, 2007: 63.

Hadjimanolis, A. (2006). A Case Study of SME-University Research Collaboration in the Context of a Small Peripheral Country (Cyprus). *International Journal of Innovation Management* 1 (10), pp. 65-88.

Hamel, G. and Prahalad, C.K. (1996). *Competing for the Future*. Boston: Harvard Business School Press.

Harrison, P. (1993). *Inside the Third World: The Anatomy of Poverty* (3rd Ed.) Middlesex, England Penguin Book Ltd.

Human Development Report (2004). By The United Nations Development Programme, New York, Oxford University Press.

Ito. K. and Rose, E.L. (2004). An Emerging Structure of Corporations. *The Multinational Business Review*. Vol. 12 No. 3, (Winter 2004), pp. 63-83.

Lundvall, B.A. (1992). National Systems of Innovation. London: Printer.

Roe, A.R., (1991). *Economy*. In Regional Survey of the World: Africa South of Sahara (1992), 21st edition, Europe Publications Limited, London.

Report on Renewable Energy (2007), Renewable Energy Sources, available at: http://www.azom.com/news.asp?news ID=6829: (Accessed: November 30, 2007)

Starbuck, E. (2002). *Innovative Activities in Swedish Firms*. NUTEK: Sweden.

Schlosser, E. (2002). *Fast Food Nation: What the All American Is Doing to the World*. London. Penguin Books Ltd.

Spiegel Special Geschichte (2007) Nr. 2, 22-05-07: 31

Svenska Dagbladet, January 18, 1989:4

Swee, G.K., (1995). *Wealth of East Asian Nations*, Singapore Federal Publications Pte. Limited.

Todaro, M.P., (1994). *Economic Development*, 5th Edition, Longman Publishing, New York.

Tucker, R, C. (2007). Industry-sponsored University Research: An Underutilized Resource. *Advanced Materials and Processes* 5 (165), pp. 78-81.

Tzokas, N. & Saren, M. (2004). Competitive Advantage, Knowledge and Relationship Marketing: Where, What and How? *Journal of Business and Industrial Marketing* 9 (1), pp. 20-42.

Williams, D.A., Wint, A. G., (2002). Attracting FDI to Developing Countries. A Changing Role for Governments? *The International Journal of Public Sector Management*, Vol. 15 No. 5, pp. 361-374.

World Development Report (1994). *Infrastructure for Development*. Published for the World Bank, Oxford/New York/Toronto, Oxford University Press.

World Development Report (1990). *Poverty,* Published for the World Bank, Oxford/New York/Toronto, Oxford University Press.

www.ingramcontent.com/pod-product-compliance
Ingram Content Group UK Ltd.
Pitfield, Milton Keynes, MK11 3LW, UK
UKHW020124200726
13856UKWH00002B/722